Woodworker's Guide to Making Traditional Mirrors and Picture Frames

By John A. Nelson

Fox
Chapel Publishing Co. Inc.

1970 Broad Street • East Petersburg, PA 17520 • www.foxchapelpublishing.com

Publisher	Alan Giagnocavo
Book Editor	Ayleen Stellhorn
Editorial Assistant	Gretchen Bacon
Desktop Specialist	Alan Davis
Cover Design	Jon Deck

ISBN 1–56523–223–2

Library of Congress Control Number 2003116144

To order your copy of this book,
please send check or money order
for the cover price plus $3.50 shipping to:
Fox Books
1970 Broad St.
East Petersburg, PA 17520
1-800-457-9112

Or visit us on the web at **www.foxchapelpublishing.com**

Printed in China

10 9 8 7 6 5 4 3 2 1

Acknowledgments

Producing a book like this requires many dedicated people. I could not have done it alone. I would like to thank the following people for their help and input.

First of all to the many early crafters who made these wonderful, original mirrors 150 to 200 years ago; to my wife Joyce, who spent hours on struggling with my poor penmanship and put it all into a readable manuscript; to David Swartz of Eagle-America for designing and developing a great set of router bits used to make the mirrors in this book; and to Warren Kafitz for his suggestions and input.

Last but not least, to Alan Giagnocavo, Ayleen Stellhorn and the dedicated staff at Fox Chapel Publishing Company of East Petersburg, Pennsylvania. I want each of you to know how much I appreciate all your efforts. Your help and support really made this book.

I hope you, our readers, like all our efforts. Any comments can be sent to me at the following address.

John A. Nelson
c/o Fox Chapel Publishing Co., Inc.
1970 Broad Street
East Petersburg, PA 17520
Editors@carvingworld.com

Contents

Mirrors

Early mirrors were called "looking glasses" and were a luxury item used by the very rich. Even years after the Revolutionary War here in America, all mirrors were imported. Our fledgling country did not have the means to manufacture mirrors at that time.

In those early days, colonists made the wood part of the mirror from local woods such as maple, cherry and walnut. They filled the mirror frames with glass shipped to the colonies from Europe.

From around 1740 to 1760, the Queen Anne style of mirror was most popular. This style featured a very plain and simple design. During the second half of the 1700s, colonists began to produce the new Chippendale "scrolled" looking glasses. This style of looking glass was popular from 1750 right up to 1800. It featured ornate scrolls, the addition of side scrolls, and the notable goose neck and flame scrolls. Today the Queen Anne and Chippendale styles are widely reproduced and are still very popular elements of home décor.

For over twenty years, I have been recording original, antique "looking glass" patterns from the New England, Pennsylvania and Ohio areas. Although these designs were handmade during different time periods, at various locations around the country and by different craftsmen, there are many similarities among them. It is almost as if the early craftsmen had a "guide book" of designs back then. Many of these mirror designs include the famous "goose neck," similar loops and identical "flame" patterns.

A simple mirror can brighten any room.

Notice that the mirror on this page features the same top scroll work as that on page 1. The author added additional scrolls and elongated the mirror to fit a narrow wall space in his home.

The 18 mirror patterns in this book are direct copies of original antiques dating from 1730 to 1885. Some of the mirrors have been scaled down by about thirty percent for use in today's smaller homes.

Next to clocks, I have found that mirrors are very popular and sell well. You can get a good price for a handmade mirror, so they make great craft sale items. After making a few mirrors, you can make a mirror in three or four hours time. Coupled with inexpensive material cost, a mirror could be a high-profit project to sell. Mirrors also make wonderful gifts.

Picture Frames

Mirror frames and picture frames have a lot in common. Like mirrors, picture frames have a top/bottom, two sides, four splines, a backboard and plain glass or mirror. Unlike mirrors, picture frames usually do not include scrolled borders.

Plain picture frames can be made to any size and to suit any need. Simple frames can be made with any extra framing material you have left over from the mirrors you have made. To make a beautiful wooden picture frame, simply follow the same steps given for making a mirror frame and eliminate the scrolls.

Mirror and Frame Designs

You will find five major styles of mirrors and frames in this book.

1. Simple mirror or picture frame without scrolls.
2. Simple mirror with scroll at top only.
3. Simple mirror with scroll at top and bottom.
4. Mirror with scroll at top and sides.
5. Mirror with scroll at top, bottom and sides.

There are eighteen specific mirror plans in

this book, but you can create any number of mirrors by slightly altering any of the plans. For example, you can enlarge or reduce each mirror to fit a particular space or need. A very easy modification involves keeping the width but lengthening the rectangular frame. You can also modify each design slightly to come up with a completely new design. Try eliminating some of the side scrolls or using only parts of those scrolls. With a little imagination, the designs you can come up with are limitless.

Wood Choice

Making the 18 reproduction mirrors featured in this book requires very little material. For this reason, I suggest that you choose wood with plenty of interesting grain patterns. As an example, if you plan to make a mirror from maple, try to find curly maple or even some Birdseye maple. The extra cost will be very little because the amount of material needed is so little.

Using top quality wood can mean the difference between a "nice" mirror and an absolutely "beautiful" mirror. Again, because very little material is actually needed in making a mirror, the extra cost to buy top quality wood is very low.

Also note that only hardwoods should be used to construct the mirror. Soft woods such as pine or spruce should be used only for the backboard.

Below is an abbreviated list of ideal woods for making mirrors and frames. Keep in mind that any quality hardwood will make a nice mirror or frame.

Walnut: A dark wood with tight grain.

Cherry: A light wood with a reddish tint and a straight grain that darkens with age.

Maple: A light wood with an obvious straight grain.

Birdseye Maple: A light wood with a curly grain and "eyes."

Tiger Maple: A light wood with a striped grain.

Mahogany: A very dark wood with a tight open grain.

This mirror is the same as that on the opposite page, except the author made this project from tiger-striped maple to match a different area of his house.

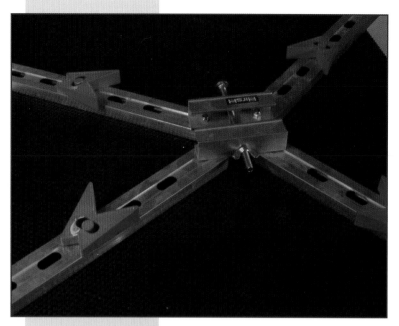

A framing jig makes clamping a frame together very easy. This jig tightens and squares all four corners simultaneously.

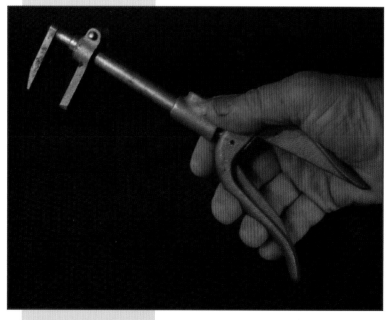

A brad driver is used to drive brads into the backing of the frame, holding the backing and the mirror in place.

Glass and mirrors

Glass and mirror materials can be cut to size by your local glass company. Check the business listings in your phone book or do an internet search for "glass cutting" or "mirror cutting."

An option to actual glass mirror is acrylic mirror. This is an excellent choice if the mirror is for a child's room or in a high traffic area. The acrylic can be easily cut with a scroll saw or band saw. Most of this acrylic can be purchased in sheets ⅛-inch thick, 12 inches by 24 inches in size.

Tools and Set-Up

Set-up time for making a mirror or a frame takes the most time. During this process you will need to attach the bit to the router, make the correct height and depth settings for the exact cut you want, attach any required safety guards, then run the wood through the router to make the molding.

Because it is almost impossible to go back later and reproduce a molding exactly, I recommend that you make enough molding for two or three mirrors at the same time while you are set up. Having the extra material will help you recover quickly from any measuring and cutting mistakes that might occur along the way. And any extra material can be used at another time for smaller mirrors and frames.

Making the molding for the reproduction mirrors in this book is simplified considerably with the set of router bits specially designed and engineered for this purpose by Eagle America (1–800–872–2511). This set of five bits will make the moldings throughout this book, exactly as shown. Other router bits can be used to make the moldings, but duplicating the exact molding may take three or four different bits and several different set-ups.

The following common woodworking tools will be needed to make the mirror. You may make want to make substitutions to this list depending on the tools that you have available in your own shop.

Scroll saw — Used to cut frets. Note that a hand fret saw could also be used to cut the simpler fret patterns in this book.

Table saw — Use to cut wood to length and width.

Router and bits — Used to cut moldings.

Miter box or cut-off saw — Used to cut 45 degree angles. Note that the table saw could also be used for this process.

Thickness planer (optional)

Thickness sander (optional)

There are a few special tools that I highly recommend. These tools will allow you to make and assemble these mirrors and picture frames easier, quicker and safer.

• Set of five specialty router bits from Eagle America as mentioned above.

• ¼-inch diameter dado cutter bit, used to cut the dados that support the scrolls in these mirrors.

• Rabbet bit, used to cut the notch in the frames for the mirror and backing.

• Hirsh self-squaring frame clamp, which equally tightens and squares all four corners with just a turn of a central wing nut.

• Brad driver, used to push in the small brads that hold the back board and mirror in place.

Five specialty bits developed by the author and crafted by Eagle America were used to create the unique moldings for the mirrors and frames in this book.

Step-By-Step

The steps to make this Chippendale Wall Mirror c. 1820 are demonstrated on the following pages. A large finished photo, the bill of materials, the pattern and the plans appear on pages 101-108. Birdseye maple was the author's wood of choice because of its highly figured grain.

The instructions given here are very basic and were developed based on the tools I have available in my shop. I suggest that you adapt these instructions to the types of tools that you have to work with in your shop. After making a few mirrors, you may find simpler methods.

Assembly Primer

Before getting started, take the time to review Figure A (Exploded View). Be sure you fully understand exactly how a frame or mirror is cut and assembled.

1. All mirrors have a frame assembly that is made up of two side frames (1), a top frame and a bottom frame (#2), and four splines (#3). The four splines give the frame more strength and are made from hardwood scraps.

2. All mirrors have mirrored glass (#4); picture frames have mirrored glass or plain glass.

3. All mirrors have a backing (#5), which is usually made from a secondary wood or scrap wood.

4. All backings are held in place with small brads or small square cut nails (#8) for authenticity.

5. Top scrolls (#9), top side scrolls (#10), bottom scrolls (#11), and bottom side scrolls (#12) are optional decorative elements.

6. Small scrap braces (#6 and #7) add support to the scrolls.

Before You Begin

• Gather the wood and hardware as listed in the bill of materials.

• Make copies of the scrolls. All of the scroll patterns in this book are full size. If the scroll pattern is shown on multiple pages, make copies of all parts and glue them together on the dotted lines. Check that the overall width of the pattern agrees with the given dimension before starting.

• Prepare the wood for the scrolls. Sand the top and bottom surfaces with medium-grit sandpaper followed by fine-grit sandpaper. Check the thickness per the drawings.

Caution: Safety guards have been removed on the tools in order to illustrate each step. Do not remove safety guards from your equipment at any time.

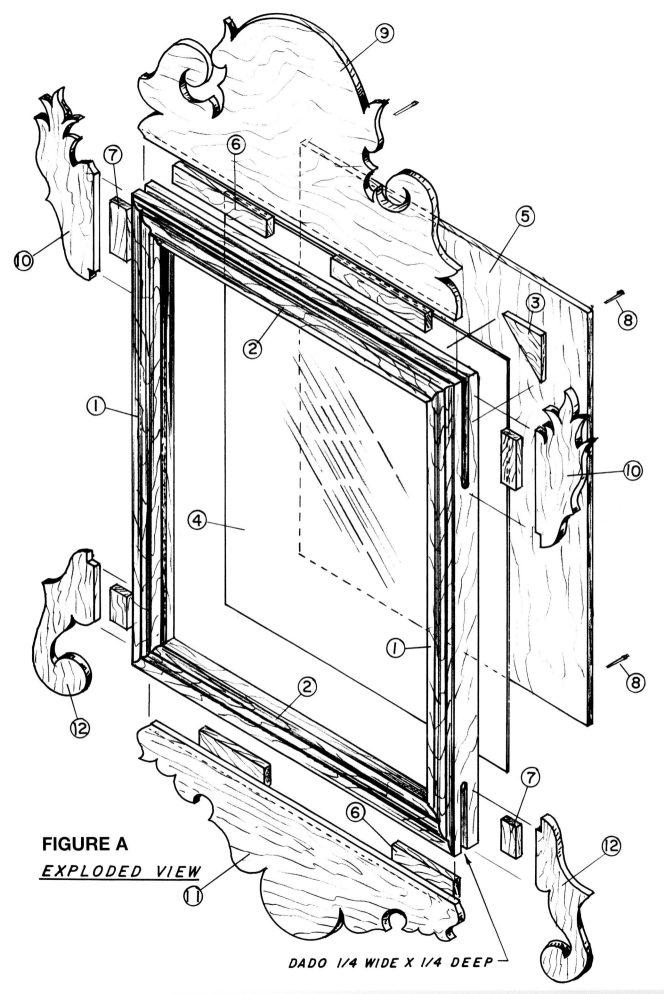

FIGURE A

EXPLODED VIEW

DADO 1/4 WIDE X 1/4 DEEP

1 Attach the pattern to the wood with spray adhesive. Be sure to spray the adhesive on the back of the pattern, not on the wood.

2 Rough cut each part into smaller pieces for easier cutting.

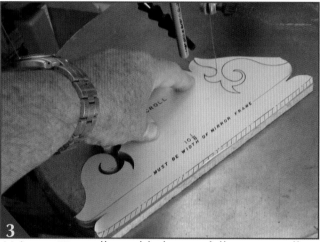

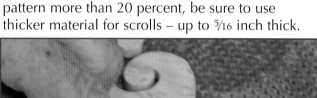

3 Using a #5 scroll saw blade, carefully cut out all the scrolls according to the pattern.
• If you want a larger mirror and if you enlarge the pattern more than 20 percent, be sure to use thicker material for scrolls – up to ⁵⁄₁₆ inch thick.

4 After cutting the scroll, sand the top and bottom surfaces using a fine- or very fine-grit sandpaper.

5 Double check that all of the pieces fit together correctly and form 90 degree angles at the corners. Mark the mating parts with a code so the parts can be easily identified and assembled later. Make any adjustments at this time.

6 Do final surface finishing with #0000 steel wool. The scrolls are now complete.

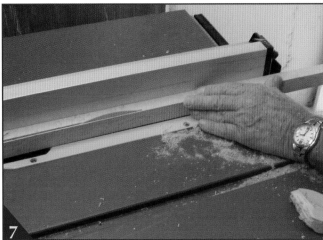

7

Cut the framing material to the overall size. Be sure all of the pieces are identical in size. Cut two or three times more material than you think you will need.

8

Using a router and the suggested bit, cut all of the molding. A molding detail shows exactly how the frame is cut. Again, cut two or three times more than you need.

9

Use either a router with a rabbet cutter bit or a table saw to cut a notch for the mirror and the backing. A table saw was used in this example. Note that the removed piece of wood could be used for braces (#7 or #8) later.

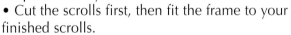

10

Carefully cut the frame top, bottom and two sides at 45 degrees. Be sure to double check and fit the top and bottom lengths with the previously cut scrolls. This is an important step and will ensure simple assembly later.
• Cut the scrolls first, then fit the frame to your finished scrolls.

11

Using a clamping jig, if you have one, glue the frame together. This handy clamping jig tightens and squares all four corners simultaneously.

12

Before the glue sets, double check that all of the corners are exactly 90 degrees. It is important to make any adjustments now, before the glue dries.

13

A simple, homemade spline cutting jig is easy to make and makes cutting the saw kerf at the four corners easier and safer. (See Figures B1, B2 and B3.)

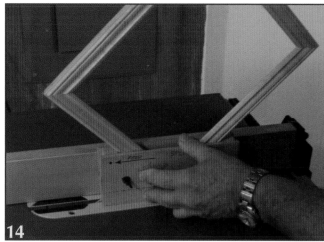

14

Using the spline cutting jig, cut a saw kerf at each of the four corners for the splines.

15

Cut four splines to saw kerf width and glue them in place. A hardwood is best for splines.

16

All four splines are glued in place.

17

Carefully cut off the overhanging 'ears' of the splines.

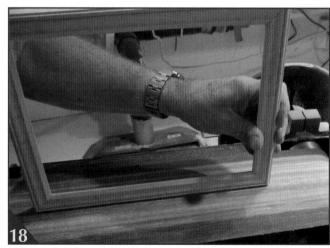

18

Sand all four edges of the frame. Be sure to keep all edges at 90 degrees from back.

19 Using a router with a ¼-inch diameter dado bit, cut the notches as needed for the scrolls. The notches are approximately ¼-inch deep. Make the cut approximately ³/₁₆ inches back from front surface. Do not try to make the ¼-inch-deep dado cut all at one time. Take ¹/₁₆-inch-deep cuts until you reach a depth of ¼ inch deep.
• Lightly mark sides of frame so you will know where to stop the side notches.

20 Sand all sides to remove any burrs.

21 Dry fit all pieces. Make any adjustments at this time, if necessary. Make sure the 45-degree angles line up. Masking tape will prevent glue from oozing onto the frame and the scroll.

22 Glue all of the scrolls in place. Use the glue sparingly and take care not get any glue on the front of the frame. Wipe off any excess glue.

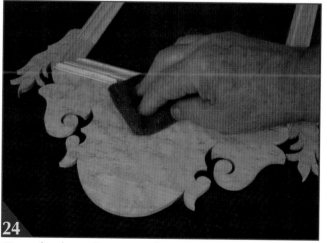

23 After the glue dries, turn the mirror over and glue braces in place as needed. Braces can be cut from scrap wood.

24 Do a final sanding over the entire surface of the mirror with #0000 steel wool or 400-grit wet sandpaper. Remove any dust with a tack rag or an air pressure hose.

25 Apply a stain of your choice. Use stain on the front and back surfaces of all of the scrolls and on the frame.

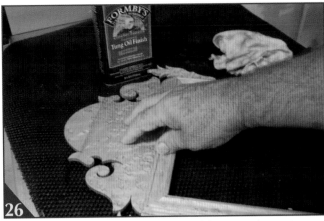

26 Add finish top coat(s) to suit. I like Formby's Tung Oil finish. I rub it by hand into the wood for that "hand rubbed" finish. Apply finish to the front and back so the scrolls will not warp. Most original antique mirrors had a satin finish; a few had a glossy finish.

27 Cut the backing to size. Adjust table saw blade to 10 degrees and carefully cut all four edges.
• After the mirror frame is assembled, turn the mirror and check the actual required size of the mirror and the backing.

28 Apply a final finish coat of wax. Rub the wax out until you get a nice "satin feel" to your mirror.

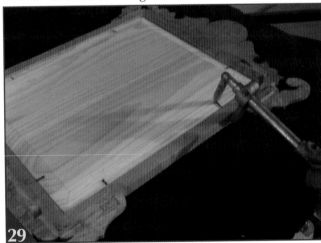

29 Turn the frame over and add the mirror and the backing. Hold the mirror and backing in place with small brads or square cut nails. A brad driver makes this task very simple.

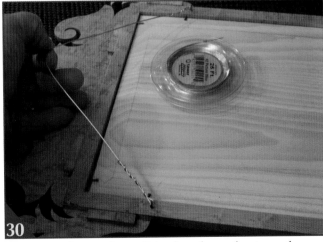

30 Measure down about 3 inches from the top of frame and attach two small screw eye loops. Add standard hanging wire, as shown. The mirror is complete and ready to hang.

Small Looking Glass
c. 1790

A simple mirror, such as this one created from zebrawood, makes an excellent addition to any room. With only one scroll at this top, this mirror makes a nice complement to any room without commanding the center of attention.

Materials List: Small Looking Glass – c. 1790

No.	Name	Size	Pieces
1	Frame, Side	3/4" x 15/16" – 8"	2
2	Frame, Top/Bottom	3/4" x 15/16" – 6 1/2"	2
3	Spline	1/8" x 1 1/2" – 3"	4
4	Mirror	5 1/8" x 6 5/8"	1
5	Backing	1/4" x 5 1/8" – 6 5/8"	1
6	Brace, Large	1/4" x 1/2" – 2 1/2"	1
7	Brace, Small	not required	
8	Nail, Square Cut	3/4" long	8
9	Top Scroll	1/4" x 4" – 6 1/2"	1
10	Side Scroll	not required	
11	Bottom Scroll	not required	
12	Side Scroll	not required	

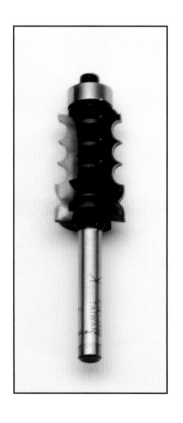

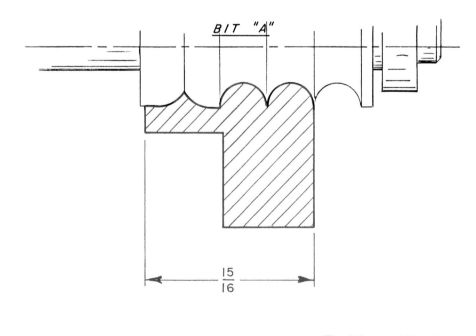

BIT "A"

$\frac{15}{16}$

Red line = Wood
Black line = Bit

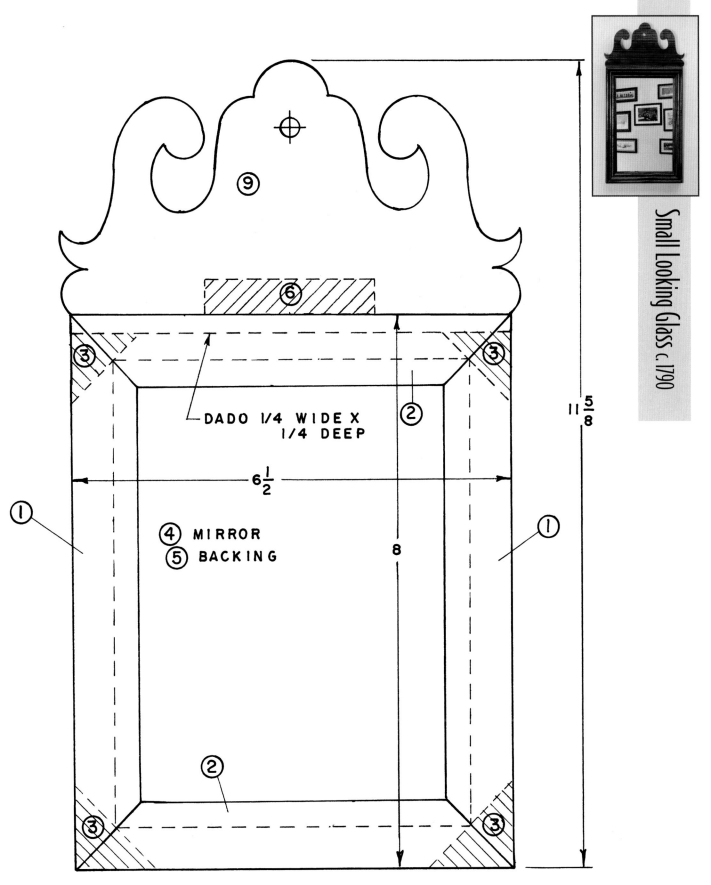

DADO 1/4 WIDE X
1/4 DEEP

⑥

⑨

③   ③

②

6 1/2

④ MIRROR
⑤ BACKING

8

① ①

11 5/8

②

③   ③

⑧ NAIL—SQUARE CUT

ASSEMBLY VIEW

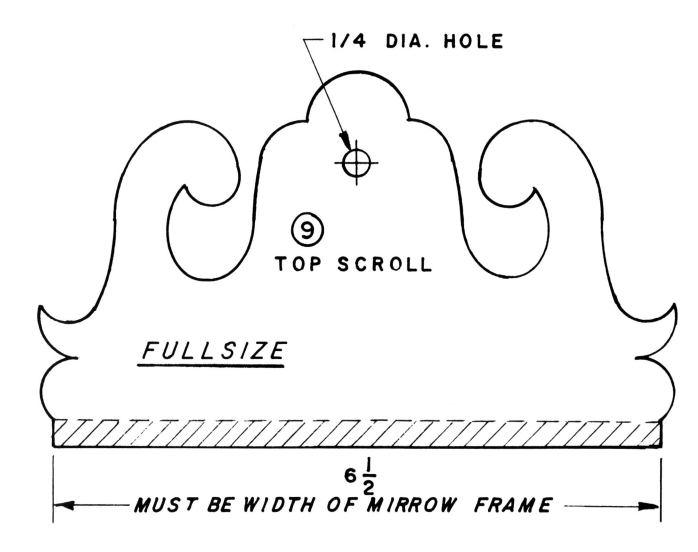

1/4 DIA. HOLE

⑨
TOP SCROLL

FULLSIZE

6 1/2
MUST BE WIDTH OF MIRROW FRAME

Early American Mirror
c. 1790

This mirror, cut from cherry, offers a wide looking glass. Placement over a vanity or a narrow chest of drawers is ideal.

Materials List: Early American Mirror – c. 1790

No.	Name	Size	Pieces
1	Frame, Side	5/8" x 7/8" – 11½"	2
2	Frame, Top/Bottom	5/8" x 7/8" – 9"	2
3	Spline	1/8" x 1½" – 3"	4
4	Mirror	8" x 10½"	1
5	Backing	¼" x 8" – 10½"	1
6	Brace, Large	¼" x ½" – 2½"	2
7	Brace, Small	not required	
8	Nail, Square Cut	¾" long	8
9	Top Scroll	¼" x 7" – 10"	1
10	Side Scroll	not required	
11	Bottom Scroll	not required	
12	Side Scroll	not required	

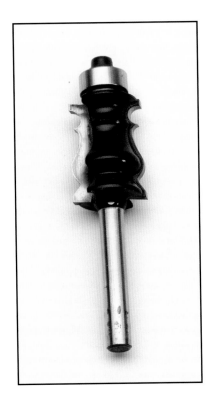

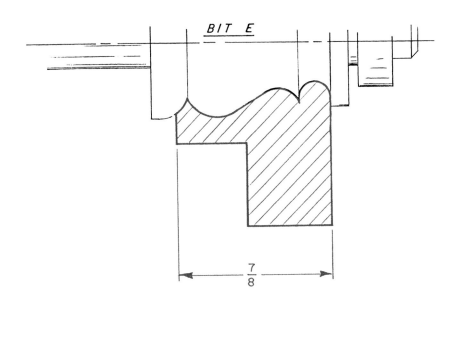

BIT E

7/8

Red line = Wood
Black line = Bit

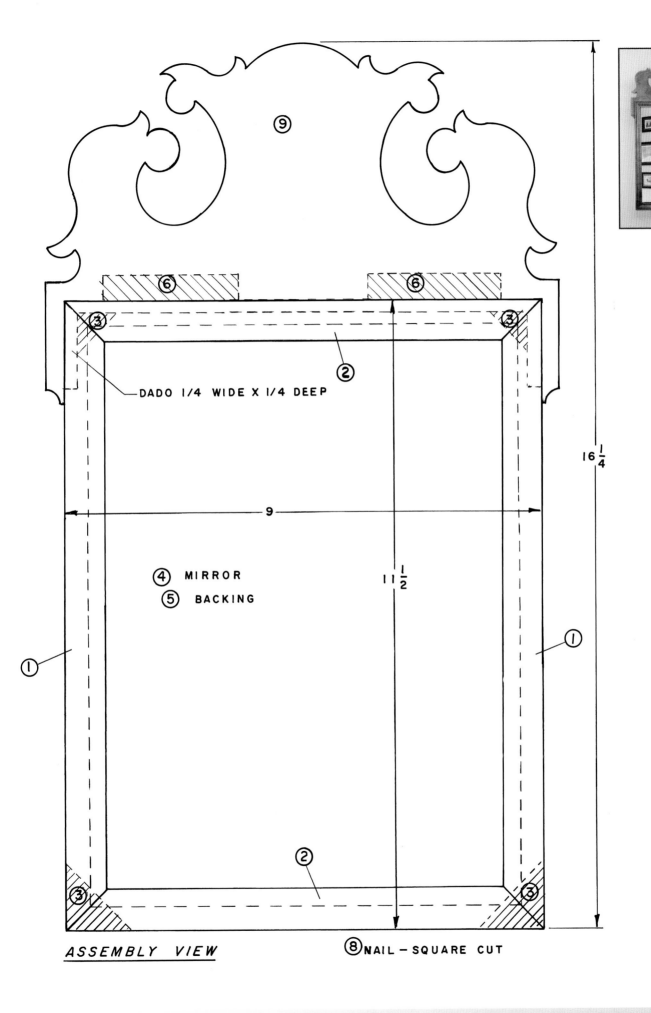

⑨

⑥   ⑥

③   ③

②

DADO 1/4 WIDE X 1/4 DEEP

16 1/4

9

① ①

④ MIRROR

⑤ BACKING

11 1/2

②

③   ③

ASSEMBLY   VIEW

⑧ NAIL — SQUARE CUT

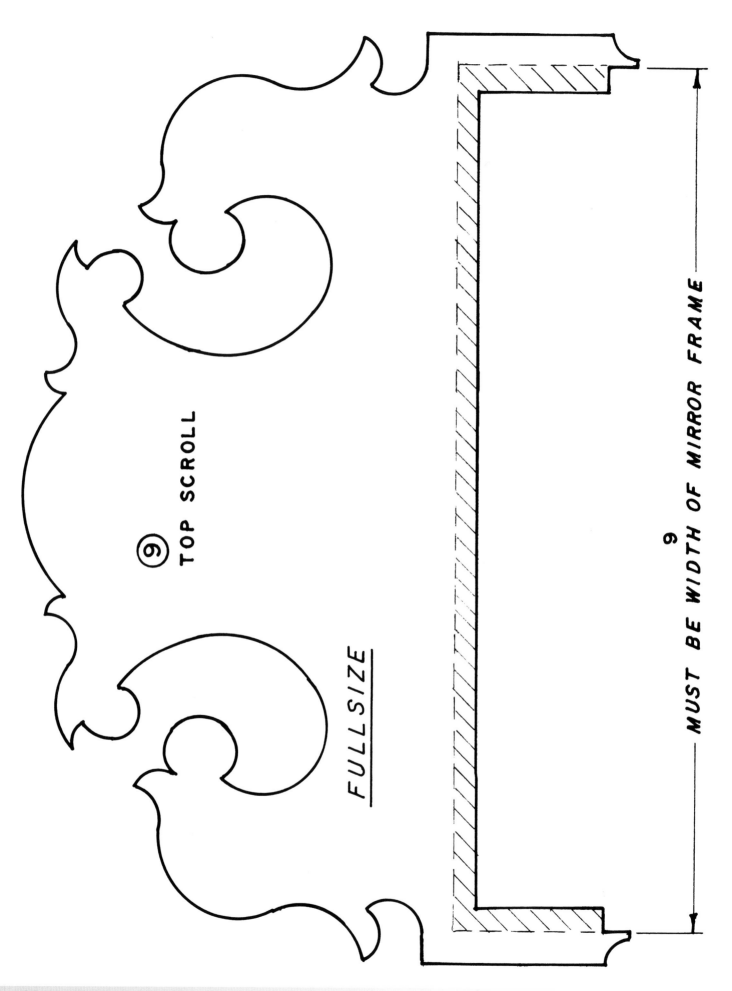

(9) TOP SCROLL

FULLSIZE

9

MUST BE WIDTH OF MIRROR FRAME

Queen Anne Mirror
c. 1730

A long, slender mirror, such as this one cut from tiger maple, makes a perfect hallway mirror. The length of the mirror can be shortened or lengthened depending on its placement in the hall.

Materials List: Queen Anne Mirror – c. 1730

No.	Name	Size	Pieces
1	Frame, Side	3/4" x 1 1/4" – 15"	2
2	Frame, Top/Bottom	3/4" x 1 1/4" – 8 1/2"	2
3	Spline	1/8" x 1 1/2" – 3"	4
4	Mirror	7 1/8" x 13 1/2"	1
5	Backing	1/4" x 7 1/8" – 13 1/2"	1
6	Brace, Large	1/4" x 1/2" – 2 1/2"	2
7	Brace, Small	not required	
8	Nail, Square Cut	3/4" long	8
9	Top Scroll	1/4" x 7" – 8 1/2"	1
10	Side Scroll	not required	
11	Bottom Scroll	not required	
12	Side Scroll	not required	

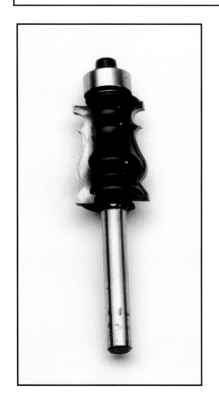

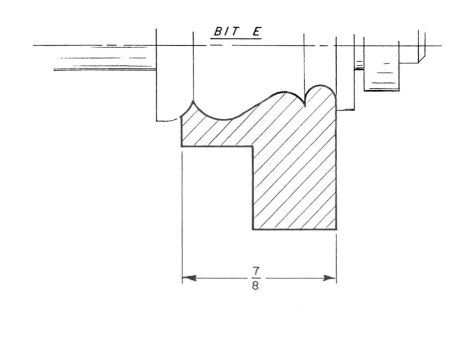

Red line = Wood
Black line = Bit

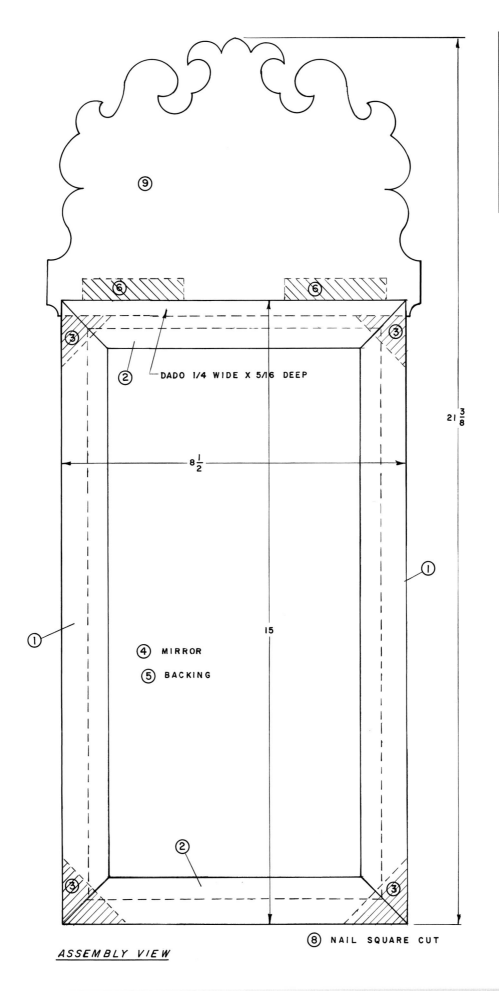

DADO 1/4 WIDE X 5/16 DEEP

② ② ③ ③ ⑥ ⑥ ⑨ ①

21 3/8

8 1/2

15

④ MIRROR

⑤ BACKING

⑧ NAIL SQUARE CUT

ASSEMBLY VIEW

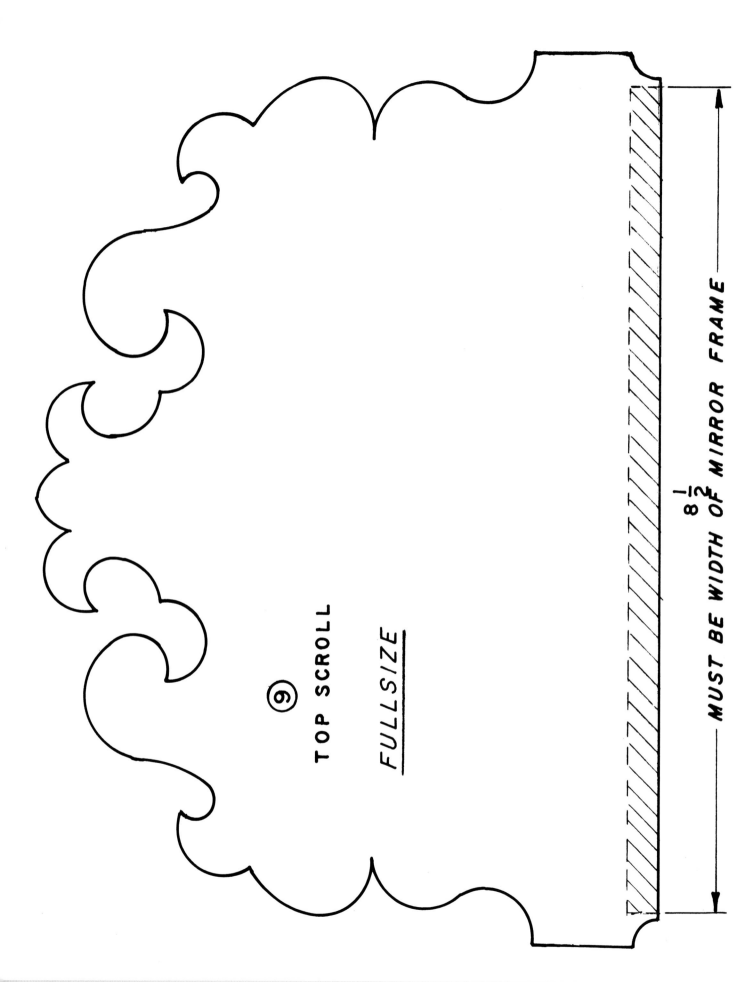

⑨ TOP SCROLL

FULLSIZE

8 ½

MUST BE WIDTH OF MIRROR FRAME

Queen Anne Mirror
c. 1745

Walnut is a dark,
domestic hardwood that
is well-suited to making
reproduction mirrors.
Here, this beautiful
wood is used to make a
simple mirror topped
with one scroll in the
Queen Anne style.

Materials List: Queen Anne Mirror – c. 1745

No.	Name	Size	Pieces
1	Frame, Side	$3/4"$ x $1^3/16"$ – 16"	2
2	Frame, Top/Bottom	$3/4"$ x $1^3/16"$ – 12 1/8"	2
3	Spline	$1/8"$ x $1^1/2"$ – 3"	4
4	Mirror	$10^5/8"$ x $14^1/2"$	1
5	Backing	$1/4"$ x $10^5/8"$ – $14^1/2"$	1
6	Brace, Large	$1/4"$ x $1/2"$ – $2^1/2"$	2
7	Brace, Small	not required	
8	Nail, Square Cut	$3/4"$ long	8
9	Top Scroll	$1/4"$ x 7" – $12^1/8"$	1
10	Side Scroll	not required	
11	Bottom Scroll	not required	
12	Side Scroll	not required	

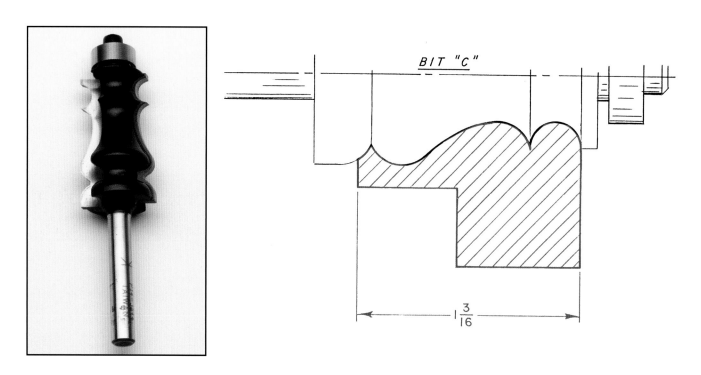

Red line = Wood
Black line = Bit

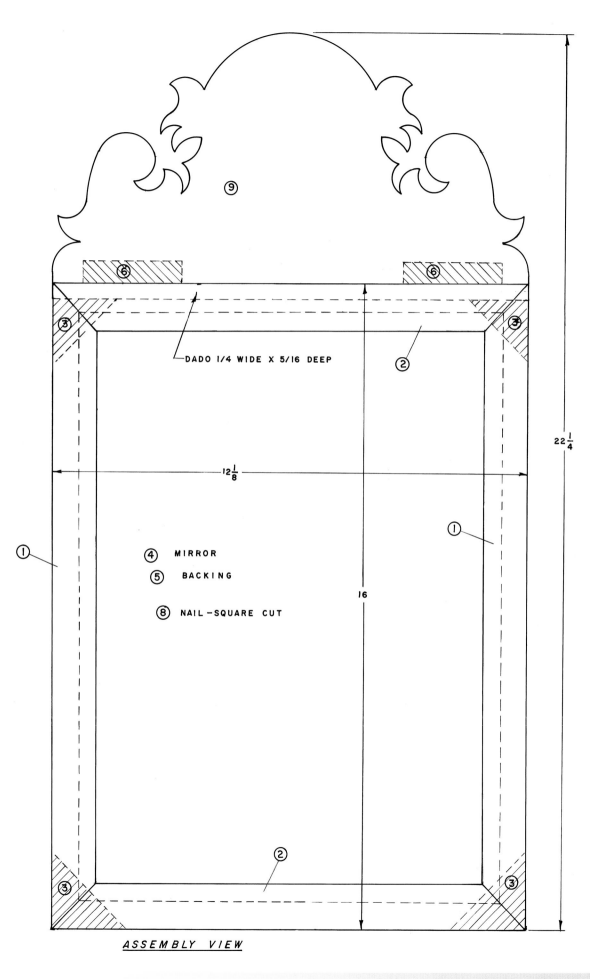

⑨

⑥   ⑥

③   ③

DADO 1/4 WIDE X 5/16 DEEP

②

22 1/4

12 1/8

16

①   ①

④ MIRROR

⑤ BACKING

⑧ NAIL—SQUARE CUT

③   ③

②

③   ③

ASSEMBLY VIEW

⑨
TOP SCROLL

12 1/4
MUST BE WIDTH OF

MIRROR FRAME

Victorian Wall Mirror
c. 1880

Victorian scrollwork tops this circa 1880 mirror cut from mahogany. Because of the ornate scrollwork, this mirror will command a visitor's attention in any room.

Materials List: Victorian Wall Mirror – c. 1880

No.	Name	Size	Pieces
1	Frame, Side	$3/4"$ x $1 1/4"$ – $15"$	2
2	Frame, Top/Bottom	$3/4"$ x $1 1/4"$ – $10 3/4"$	2
3	Spline	$1/8"$ x $1 1/2"$ – $3"$	4
4	Mirror	$9 1/4"$ x $13 5/8"$	1
5	Backing	$1/4"$ x $9 1/4"$ – $13 5/8"$	1
6	Brace, Large	$1/4"$ x $1/2"$ – $2 1/2"$	2
7	Brace, Small	not required	
8	Nail, Square Cut	$3/4"$ long	8
9	Top Scroll	$1/4"$ x $8"$ – $10 3/4"$	1
10	Side Scroll	not required	
11	Bottom Scroll	not required	
12	Side Scroll	not required	

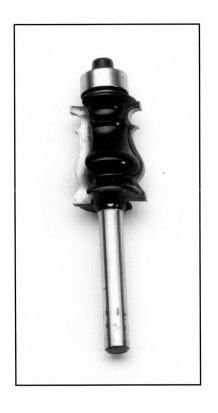

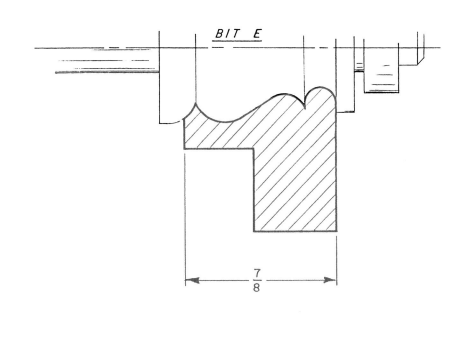

BIT E

$\dfrac{7}{8}$

Red line = Wood
Black line = Bit

⑨

TOP SCROLL

10 3/4

MUST BE WIDTH OF MIRROR FRAME

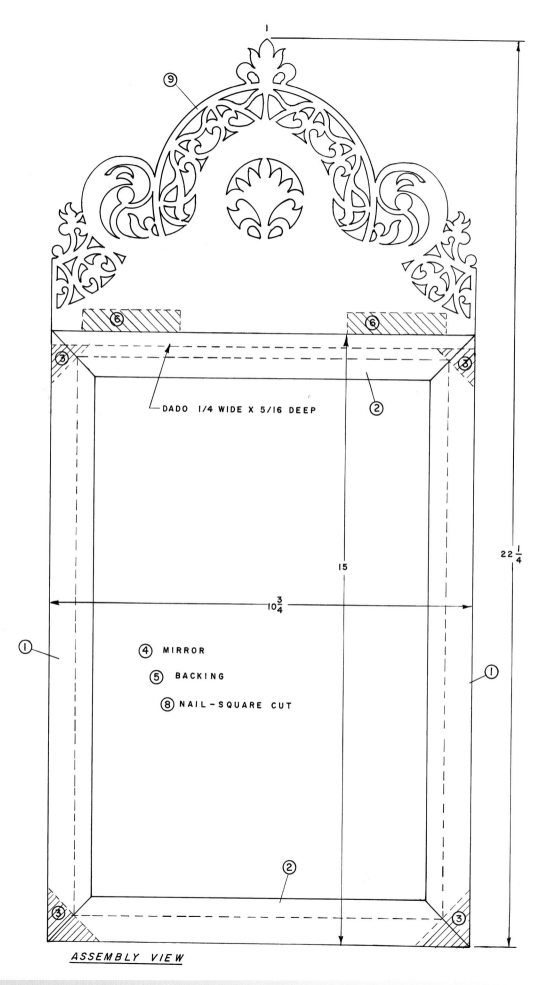

DADO 1/4 WIDE X 5/16 DEEP

15

10¾

22¼

④ MIRROR

⑤ BACKING

⑧ NAIL-SQUARE CUT

ASSEMBLY VIEW

Scroll Hall Mirror
c. 1880

Intricate scrollwork adds to the beauty of this reproduction mirror. The frame and the scrollwork were cut from tiger maple.

Materials List: Scroll Hall Mirror – c. 1880

No.	Name	Size	Pieces
1	Frame, Side	3/4" x 1 1/4" – 22"	2
2	Frame, Top/Bottom	3/4" x 1 1/4" – 16"	2
3	Spline	1/8" x 1 1/2" – 3"	4
4	Mirror	14 3/8" x 18 3/8"	1
5	Backing	1/4" x 14 3/8" – 18 3/8"	1
6	Brace, Large	1/4" x 1/2" – 2 1/2"	2
7	Brace, Small	not required	
8	Nail, Square Cut	3/4" long	8
9	Top Scroll	1/4" x 7" – 16"	1
10	Side Scroll	not required	
11	Bottom Scroll	not required	
12	Side Scroll	not required	

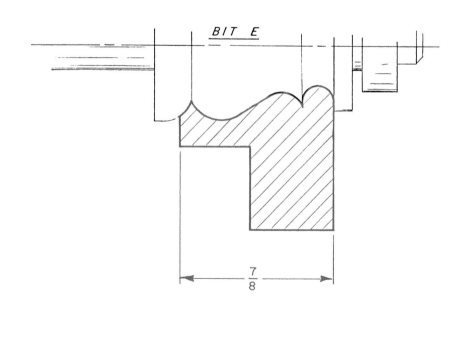

BIT E

$\frac{7}{8}$

Red line = Wood
Black line = Bit

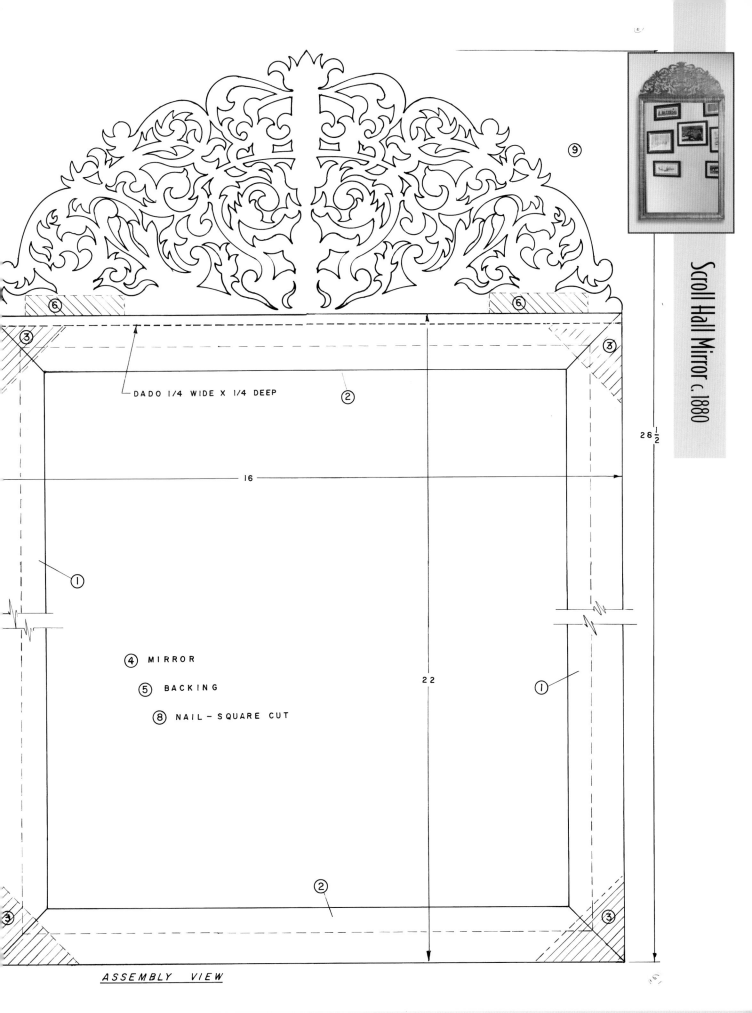

DADO 1/4 WIDE X 1/4 DEEP

② ⑨

28½

16

④ MIRROR

⑤ BACKING

22

⑧ NAIL-SQUARE CUT

①

②

③

③

③

③

⑥ ⑥

①

ASSEMBLY VIEW

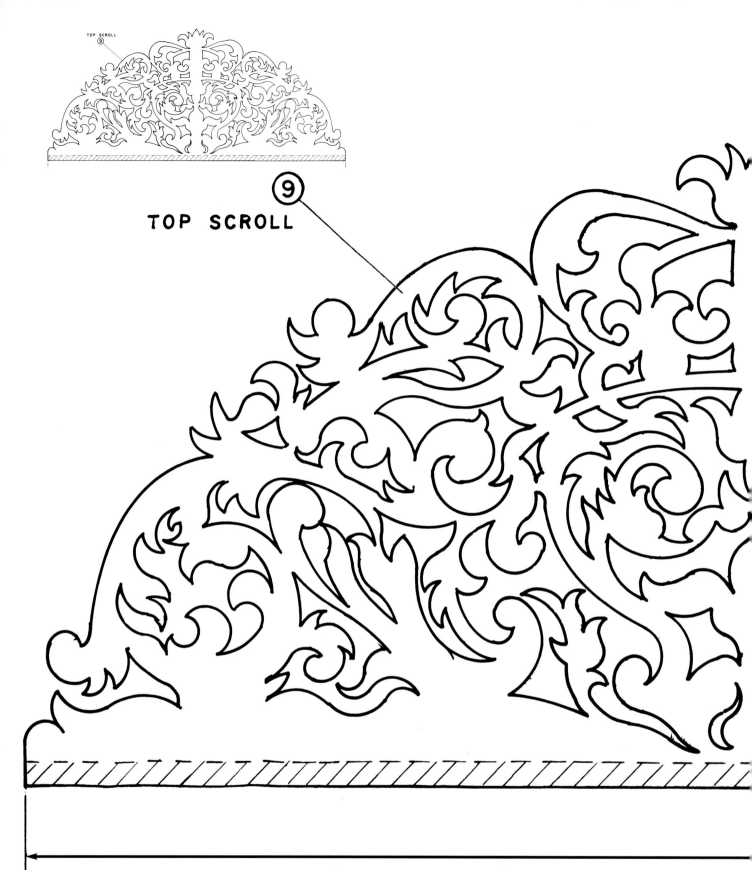

TOP SCROLL

⑨

TOP SCROLL

MUST BE WIDTH OF MIRROR FRAME

16

Early Looking Glass
c. 1800

Adding a scroll to the top and one to the bottom of the mirror frame lends a balanced look and elongates the mirror. The frame of this circa 1800 mirror is cut from tiger maple; the scrolls are bird's eye maple.

Materials List: Early Looking Glass – c. 1800

No.	Name	Size	Pieces
1	Frame, Side	$5/8$" x $11/16$" – $91/4$"	2
2	Frame, Top/Bottom	$5/8$" x $11/16$" – $71/4$"	2
3	Spline	$1/8$" x $11/2$" – 3"	4
4	Mirror	6" x $81/16$"	1
5	Backing	$1/4$" x 6" – $81/16$"	1
6	Brace, Large	$1/4$" x $1/2$" – $21/2$"	2
7	Brace, Small	not required	
8	Nail, Square Cut	$3/4$" long	8
9	Top Scroll	$1/4$" x 4" – $71/4$"	1
10	Side Scroll	not required	
11	Bottom Scroll	$1/4$" x $21/2$" – $71/4$"	1
12	Side Scroll	not required	

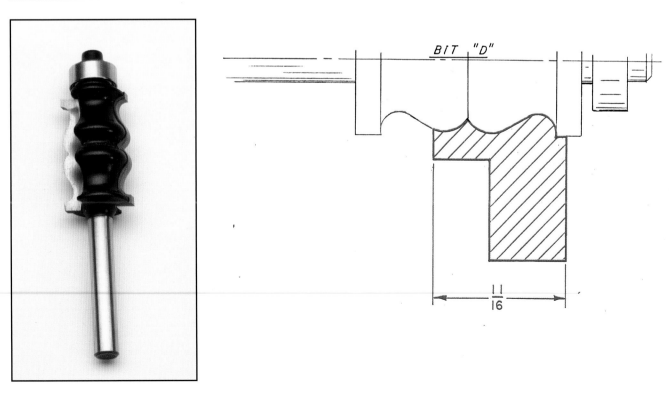

Red line = Wood
Black line = Bit

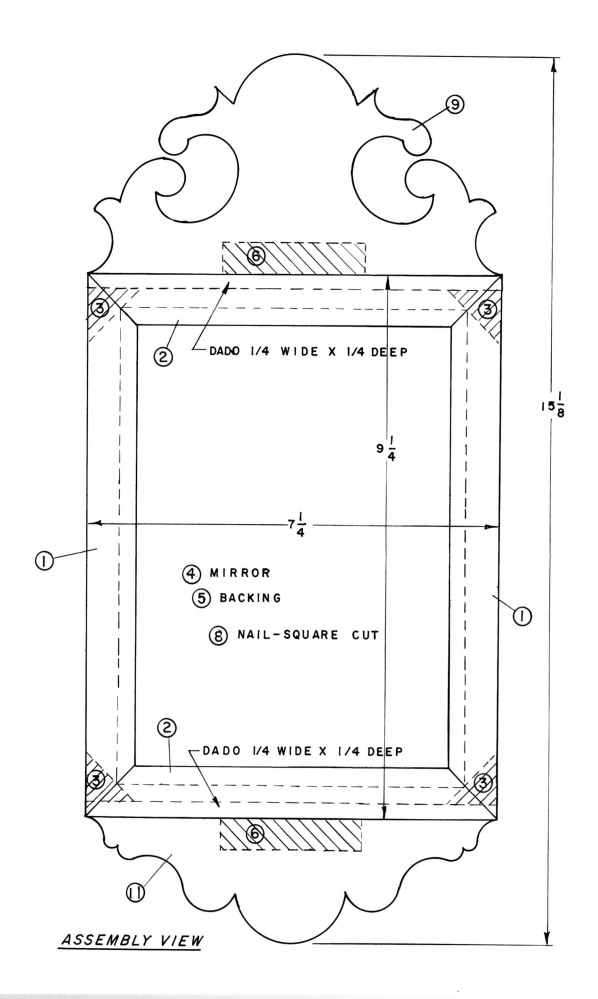

DADO 1/4 WIDE X 1/4 DEEP

DADO 1/4 WIDE X 1/4 DEEP

④ MIRROR
⑤ BACKING
⑧ NAIL-SQUARE CUT

$15\frac{1}{8}$

$9\frac{1}{4}$

$7\frac{1}{4}$

ASSEMBLY VIEW

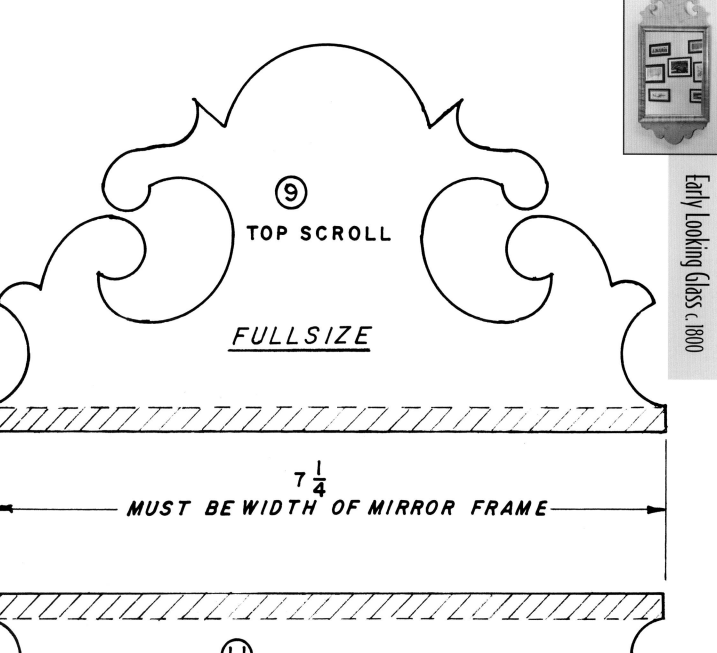

⑨

TOP SCROLL

FULLSIZE

$7\frac{1}{4}$

MUST BE WIDTH OF MIRROR FRAME

⑪

BOTTOM SCROLL

Mixing woods can enhance the look of a finished mirror. Here, maple was used for the scrolls and tiger maple was used for the frame of this large, wide mirror.

Materials List: Hall Mirror – c. 1820

No.	Name	Size	Pieces
1	Frame, Side	$5/8" \times {}^{11}/16" - 11"$	2
2	Frame, Top/Bottom	$5/8" \times {}^{11}/16" - 8"$	2
3	Spline	$1/8" \times 1^{1}/2" - 3"$	4
4	Mirror	$7" \times 10"$	1
5	Backing	$1/4" \times 7" - 10"$	1
6	Brace, Large	$1/4" \times 1/2" - 2^{1}/2"$	2
7	Brace, Small	not required	
8	Nail, Square Cut	$3/4"$ long	8
9	Top Scroll	$1/4" \times 4^{1}/8" - 8"$	1
10	Side Scroll	not required	
11	Bottom Scroll	$1/4" \times 3^{1}/8" - 8$	1
12	Side Scroll	not required	

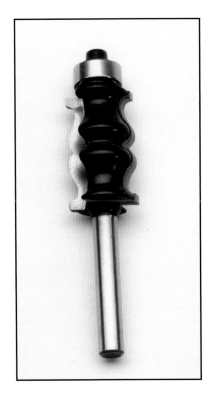

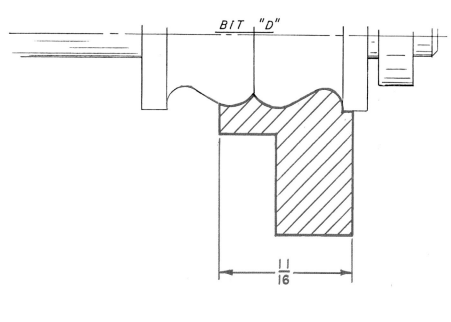

BIT "D"

$\frac{11}{16}$

Red line = Wood
Black line = Bit

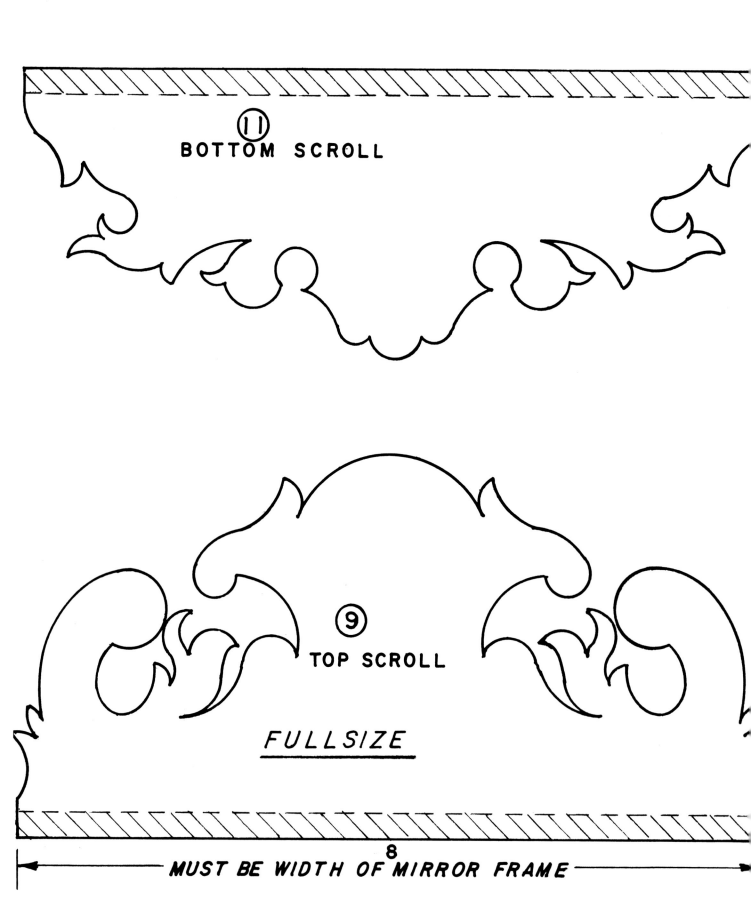

⑪
BOTTOM SCROLL

⑨
TOP SCROLL

FULLSIZE

8
◄— MUST BE WIDTH OF MIRROR FRAME —►

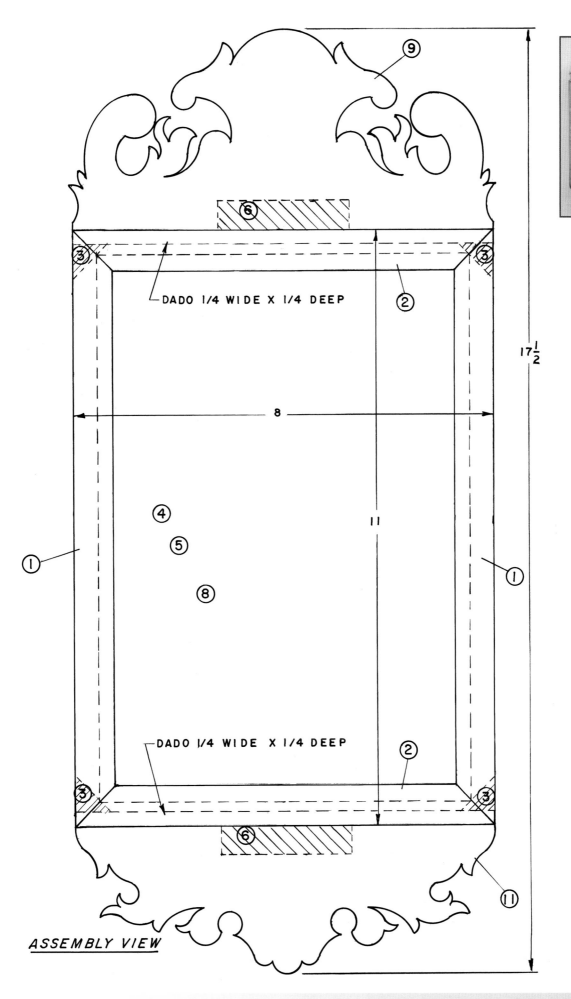

⑨

⑥

③   ③

DADO 1/4 WIDE X 1/4 DEEP   ②

17½

8

11

④

⑤

①   ①

⑧

DADO 1/4 WIDE X 1/4 DEEP   ②

③   ③

⑥

⑪

ASSEMBLY VIEW

Hall Mirror c. 1820

Bird Looking Glass
c. 1790

Tall and narrow, this double scroll mirror is perfect for a tight wall space. The scrolls were cut from maple. Tiger maple was used for the frame.

Materials List: Bird Looking Glass – c. 1790

No.	Name	Size	Pieces
1	Frame, Side	3/4" x $^{11}/_{16}$" – 13$^1/_2$"	2
2	Frame, Top/Bottom	3/4" x $^{11}/_{16}$" – 8$^5/_8$"	2
3	Spline	$^1/_8$" x 1$^1/_2$" – 3"	4
4	Mirror	7$^3/_8$" x 12$^3/_8$"	1
5	Backing	$^1/_4$" x 7$^3/_8$" – 12$^3/_8$"	1
6	Brace, Large	$^1/_4$" x $^1/_2$" – 2$^1/_2$"	3
7	Brace, Small	not required	
8	Nail, Square Cut	3/4" long	8
9	Top Scroll	$^1/_4$" x 6" – 8$^3/_4$"	1
10	Side Scroll	not required	
11	Bottom Scroll	$^1/_4$" x 2$^1/_2$" – 8$^3/_4$"	1
12	Side Scroll	not required	

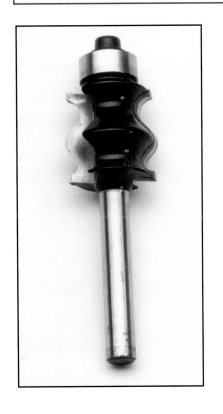

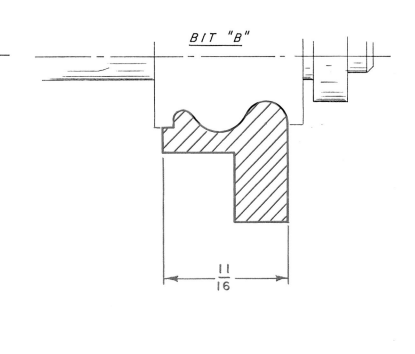

BIT "B"

$\frac{11}{16}$

Red line = Wood
Black line = Bit

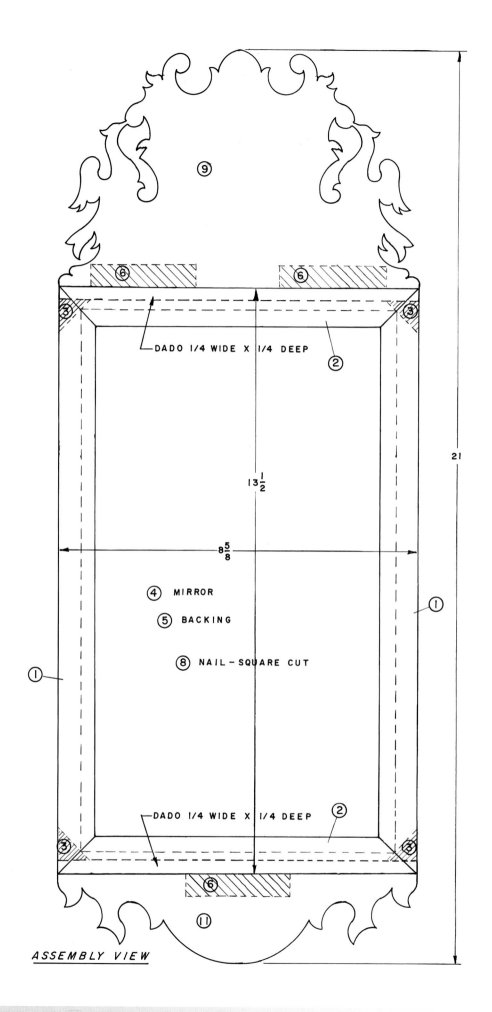

DADO 1/4 WIDE X 1/4 DEEP

② ③

$13\frac{1}{2}$

$8\frac{5}{8}$

④ MIRROR

⑤ BACKING

⑧ NAIL—SQUARE CUT

①

②

DADO 1/4 WIDE X 1/4 DEEP

21

ASSEMBLY VIEW

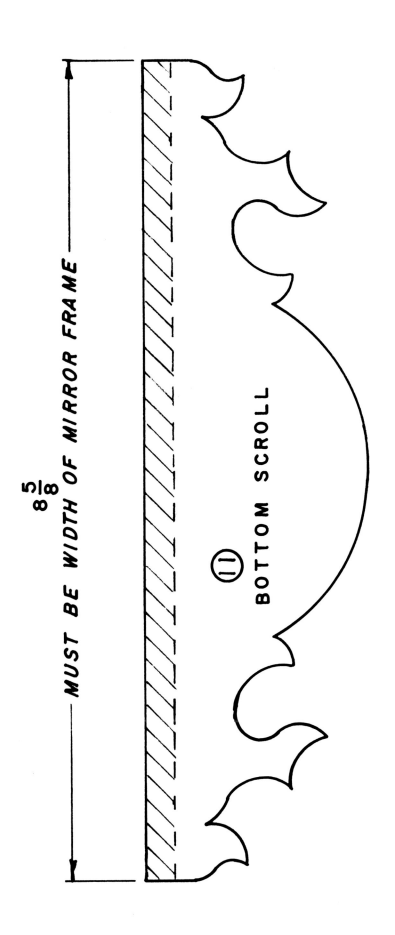

$8\frac{5}{8}$

MUST BE WIDTH OF MIRROR FRAME

BOTTOM SCROLL

Bird Looking Glass c. 1790

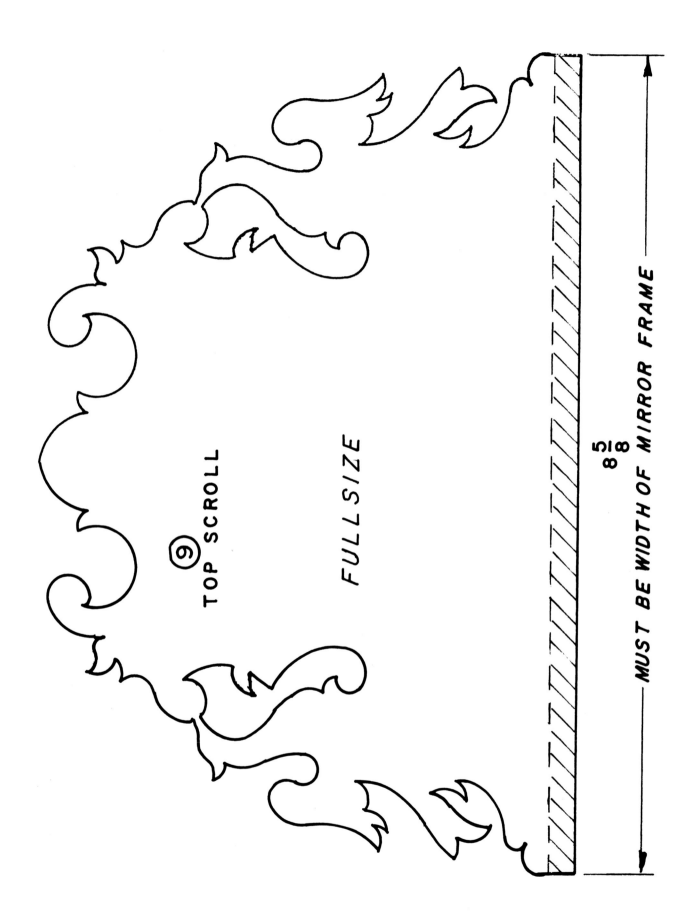

⑥ TOP SCROLL

FULL SIZE

$8\frac{5}{8}$

MUST BE WIDTH OF MIRROR FRAME

Early American Fish Tail Mirror

c. 1790

A dark stain can dramatically alter the look of a finished mirror. Here maple, normally a light-colored wood, was given a totally different appearance with the artist's use of a dark stain.

Materials List: Early American Fish Tail Mirror – c. 1790

No.	Name	Size	Pieces
1	Frame, Side	$5/8$" x $11/16$" – 14"	2
2	Frame, Top/Bottom	$5/8$" x $11/16$" – $7^3/4$"	2
3	Spline	$1/8$" x $1^1/2$" – 3"	4
4	Mirror	$6^3/4$" x 13"	1
5	Backing	$1/4$" x $6^3/4$" – 13"	1
6	Brace, Large	$1/4$" x $1/2$" – $2^1/2$"	2
7	Brace, Small	not required	
8	Nail, Square Cut	$3/4$" long	8
9	Top Scroll	$1/4$" x $6^1/2$" – 8"	1
10	Side Scroll	not required	
11	Bottom Scroll	$1/4$" x 3" – 8"	1
12	Side Scroll	not required	

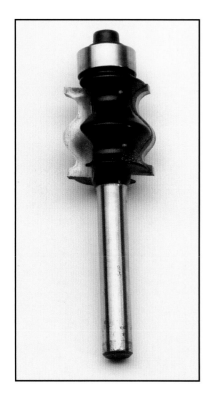

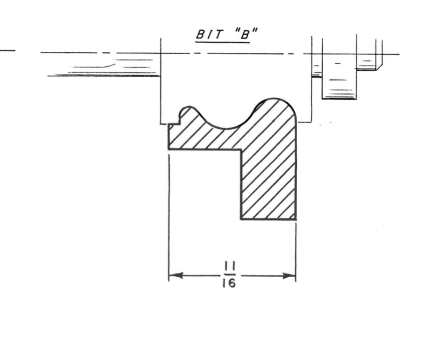

BIT "B"

$\frac{11}{16}$

Red line = Wood
Black line = Bit

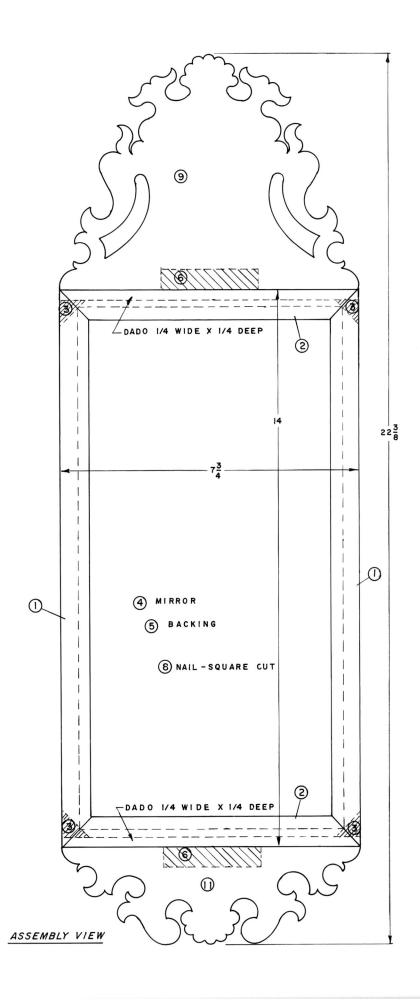

DADO 1/4 WIDE X 1/4 DEEP

②

14

7 3/4

22 3/8

④ MIRROR

⑤ BACKING

⑧ NAIL - SQUARE CUT

②

DADO 1/4 WIDE X 1/4 DEEP

⑥

⑪

ASSEMBLY VIEW

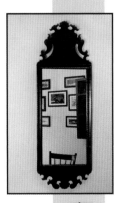

⑨

TOP SCROLL

FULLSIZE

$7\frac{3}{4}$

MUST BE WIDTH OF MIRROR FRAME

⑪

BOTTOM SCROLL

Victorian Wall Mirror
c. 1865

This Victorian-style hall mirror incorporates lacey scrollwork on three sides: top, left and right. The grain of tiger maple lends interest to the broad top scroll and the frame.

Materials List: Victorian Wall Mirror – c. 1865

No.	Name	Size	Pieces
1	Frame, Side	$5/8$" x $15/16$" – 17"	2
2	Frame, Top/Bottom	$5/8$" x $15/16$" – $8^1/8$"	2
3	Spline	$1/8$" x $1^1/2$" – 3"	4
4	Mirror	$7^1/8$" x $15^7/8$"	1
5	Backing	$1/4$" x $7 \ ^1/8$" – $15^7/8$"	1
6	Brace, Large	$1/4$" x $1/2$" – $2^1/2$"	1
7	Brace, Small	not required	
8	Nail, Square Cut	$3/4$" long	8
9	Top Scroll	$1/4$" x $4^1/4$" – $8^1/4$"	1
10	Side Scroll	$1/4$" x $1^1/2$" – $7^1/2$"	2
11	Bottom Scroll	not required	
12	Side Scroll	$1/4$" x $1^1/4$" – $5^1/4$"	2

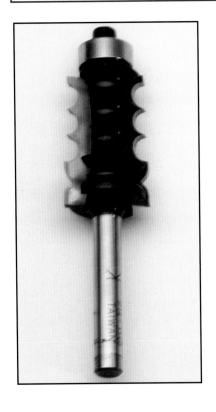

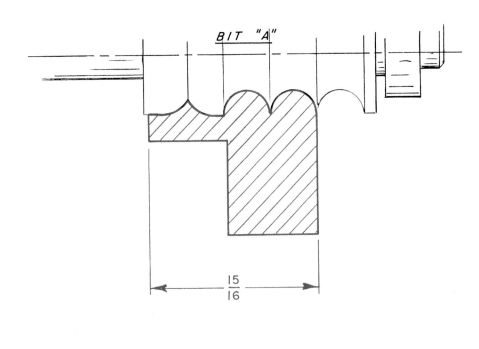

BIT "A"

$\frac{15}{16}$

Red line = Wood
Black line = Bit

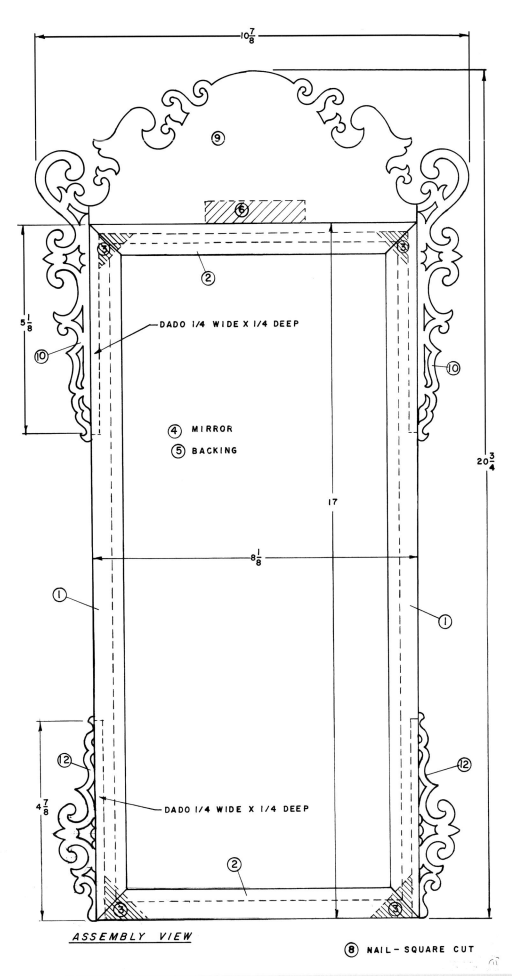

10⅞

⑨

⑥

⑤   ⑤

2

DADO 1/4 WIDE X 1/4 DEEP

5⅛

⑩   ⑩

④ MIRROR
⑤ BACKING

20¾

17

①   ①

8⅛

⑫   ⑫

4⅞

DADO 1/4 WIDE X 1/4 DEEP

②

ASSEMBLY VIEW

⑧ NAIL – SQUARE CUT

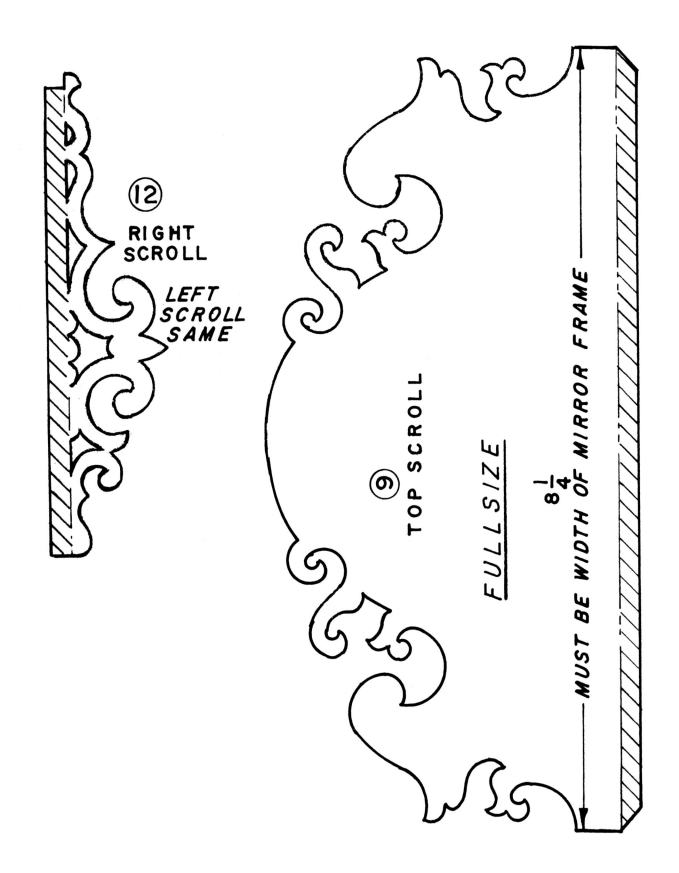

12
RIGHT
SCROLL

LEFT
SCROLL
SAME

9
TOP SCROLL

FULLSIZE

$8\frac{1}{4}$

MUST BE WIDTH OF MIRROR FRAME

⑩
LEFT
SCROLL

⑩
RIGHT
SCROLL

Hall Mirror
c. 1790

The whorls of bird's eye maple provide an interesting grain for this mirror. Scrolls were included on all four sides of this hall mirror.

Materials List: Hall Mirror – c. 1790

No.	Name	Size	Pieces
1	Frame, Side	$3/4$" x $^{11}/_{16}$" – 15"	2
2	Frame, Top/Bottom	$3/4$" x $^{11}/_{16}$" – $6^{5}/_{8}$"	2
3	Spline	$1/8$" x $1^{1}/_{2}$" – 3"	4
4	Mirror	$5^{7}/_{16}$" x $13^{5}/_{8}$"	1
5	Backing	$1/4$" x $5^{7}/_{16}$" – $13^{5}/_{8}$"	1
6	Brace, Large	$1/4$" x $1/2$" – $2^{1}/_{2}$"	2
7	Brace, Small	$1/4$" x $1/2$" – $1^{1}/_{4}$"	4
8	Nail, Square Cut	$3/4$" long	8
9	Top Scroll	$1/4$" x $4^{1}/_{2}$" – $6^{3}/_{4}$"	1
10	Side Scroll	$1/4$" x $1^{1}/_{2}$" – $6^{1}/_{4}$"	2
11	Bottom Scroll	$1/4$" x $3^{1}/_{2}$" – $7^{1}/_{8}$"	1
12	Side Scroll	$1/4$" x $1^{1}/_{2}$" – $5^{1}/_{2}$"	2

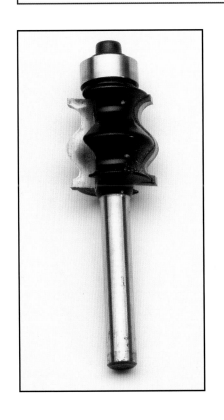

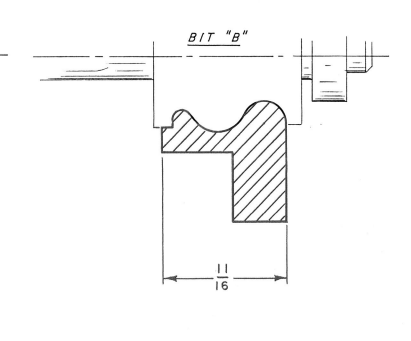

BIT "B"

$\frac{11}{16}$

Red line = Wood
Black line = Bit

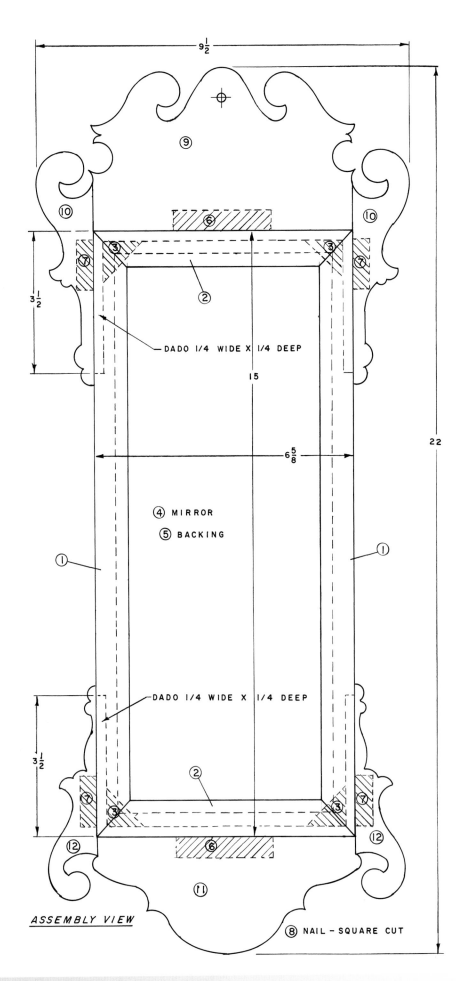

$9\frac{1}{2}$

⑨

⑩   ⑩

⑥

③   ③

⑦   ⑦

$3\frac{1}{2}$

②

DADO 1/4 WIDE X 1/4 DEEP

15

22

$6\frac{5}{8}$

④ MIRROR

⑤ BACKING

①   ①

DADO 1/4 WIDE X 1/4 DEEP

$3\frac{1}{2}$

②

⑦   ⑦

③   ③

⑫   ⑫

⑥

⑪

ASSEMBLY VIEW

⑧ NAIL — SQUARE CUT

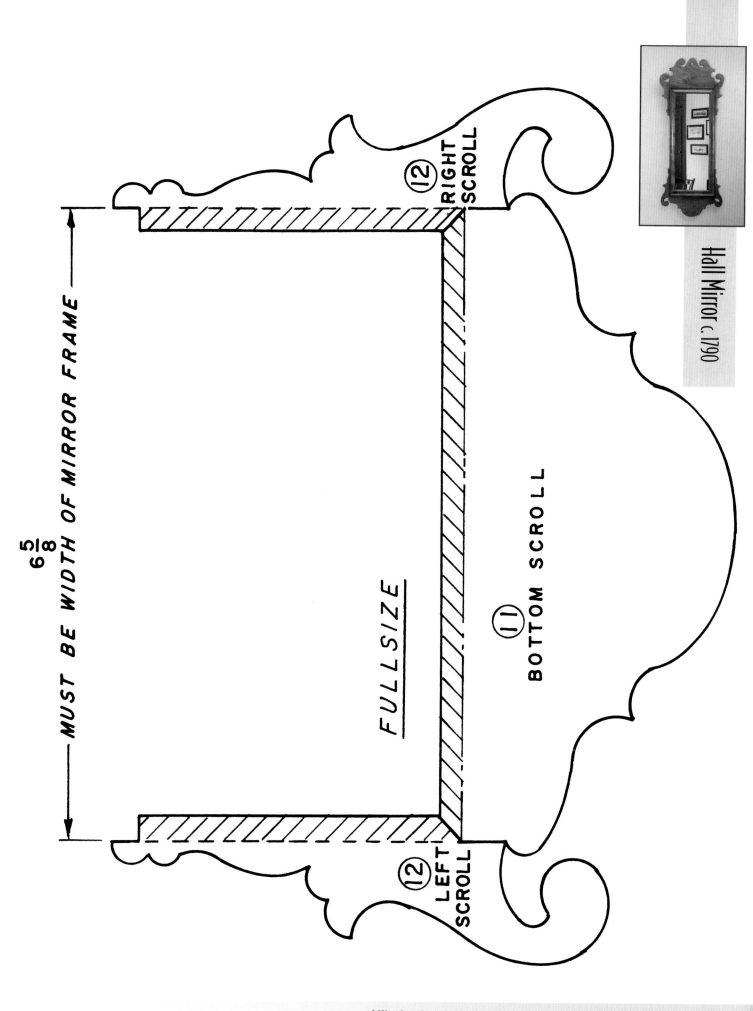

$6\frac{5}{8}$

MUST BE WIDTH OF MIRROR FRAME

12 RIGHT SCROLL

FULLSIZE

BOTTOM SCROLL

11

12 LEFT SCROLL

Hall Mirror c. 1790

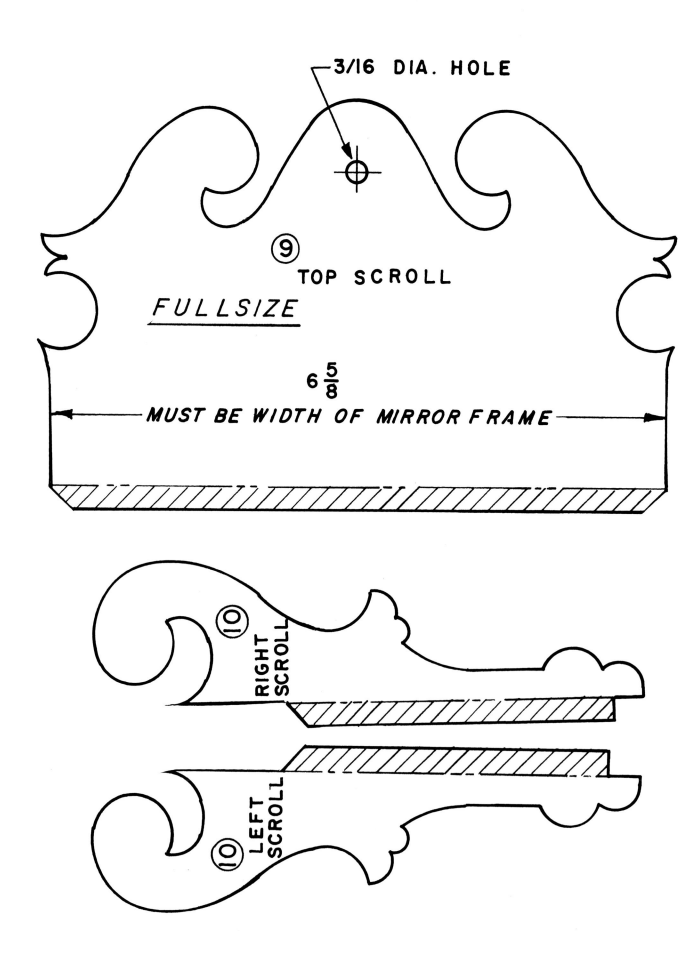

3/16 DIA. HOLE

⑨ TOP SCROLL

FULLSIZE

$6\frac{5}{8}$

← MUST BE WIDTH OF MIRROR FRAME →

⑩ RIGHT SCROLL

⑩ LEFT SCROLL

Chippendale Mirror
c. 1780

This Chippendale-style reproduction, cut from tiger maple, features small scrolls on the sides that continue the flow lines of the top and bottom scrolls.

Materials List: Chippendale Mirror – c. 1780

No.	Name	Size	Pieces
1	Frame, Side	$^{3}/_{4}$" x $^{15}/_{16}$" – 12$^{5}/_{8}$"	2
2	Frame, Top/Bottom	$^{3}/_{4}$" x $^{15}/_{16}$" – 7$^{3}/_{8}$"	2
3	Spline	$^{1}/_{8}$" x 1$^{1}/_{2}$" – 3"	4
4	Mirror	6" x 11$^{3}/_{8}$"	1
5	Backing	$^{1}/_{4}$" x 6" – 11 $^{3}/_{8}$"	1
6	Brace, Large	$^{1}/_{4}$" x $^{1}/_{2}$" – 2$^{1}/_{2}$"	2
7	Brace, Small	not required	
8	Nail, Square Cut	$^{3}/_{4}$" long	8
9	Top Scroll	$^{1}/_{4}$" x 4" – 7$^{1}/_{2}$"	1
10	Side Scroll	$^{1}/_{4}$" x 1$^{1}/_{8}$" – 4"	2
11	Bottom Scroll	$^{1}/_{4}$" x 3" – 7$^{1}/_{2}$"	1
12	Side Scroll	$^{1}/_{4}$" x 1$^{1}/_{4}$" – 4"	2

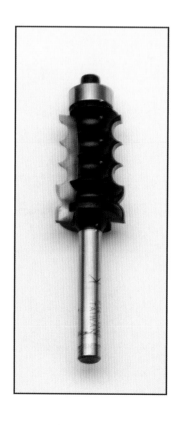

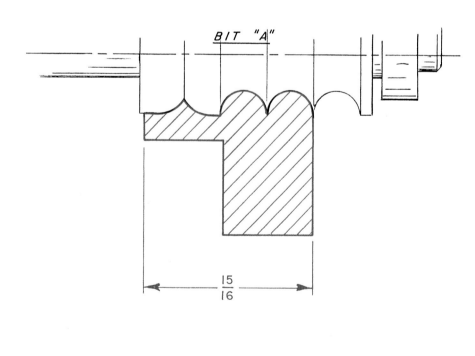

Red line = Wood
Black line = Bit

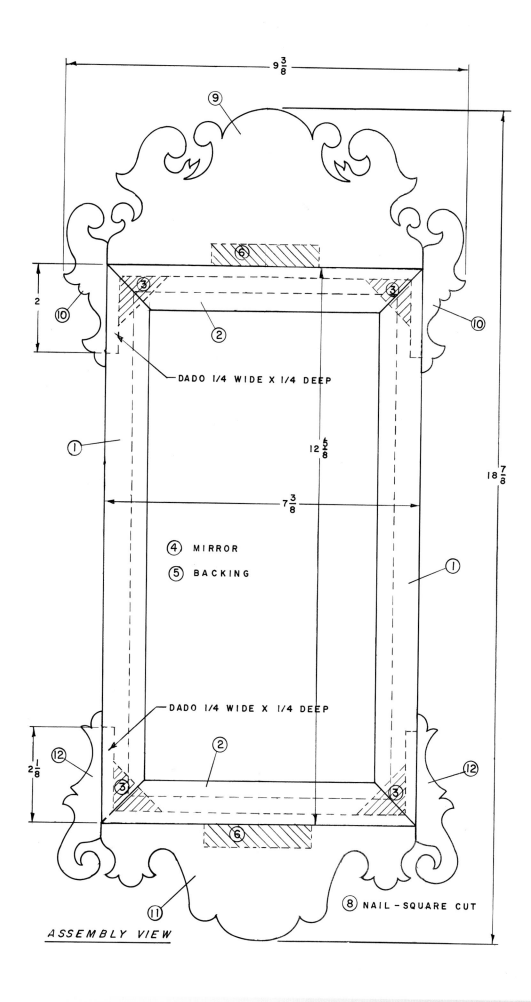

$9\frac{3}{8}$

⑨

② DADO 1/4 WIDE X 1/4 DEEP

⑥

③   ③

⑩   ⑩

2

①

$12\frac{5}{8}$

$18\frac{7}{8}$

$7\frac{3}{8}$

①

④ MIRROR
⑤ BACKING

DADO 1/4 WIDE X 1/4 DEEP

②

$2\frac{1}{8}$ ③   ③

⑫   ⑫

⑥

⑧ NAIL–SQUARE CUT

⑪

ASSEMBLY VIEW

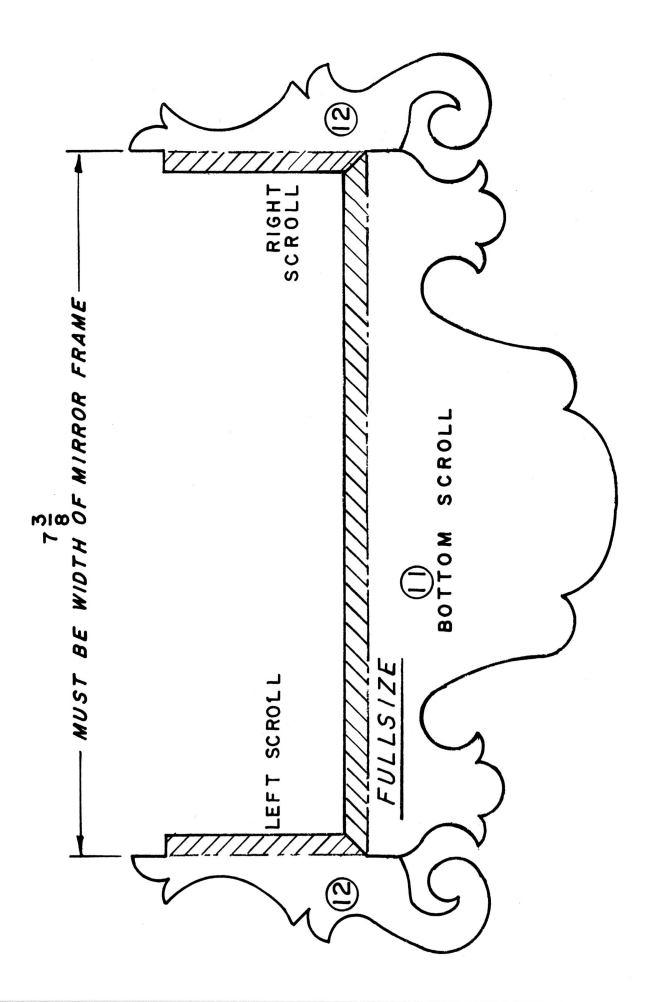

RIGHT SCROLL

LEFT SCROLL

BOTTOM SCROLL

⑪

⑫

⑫

FULLSIZE

$7\frac{3}{8}$

MUST BE WIDTH OF MIRROR FRAME

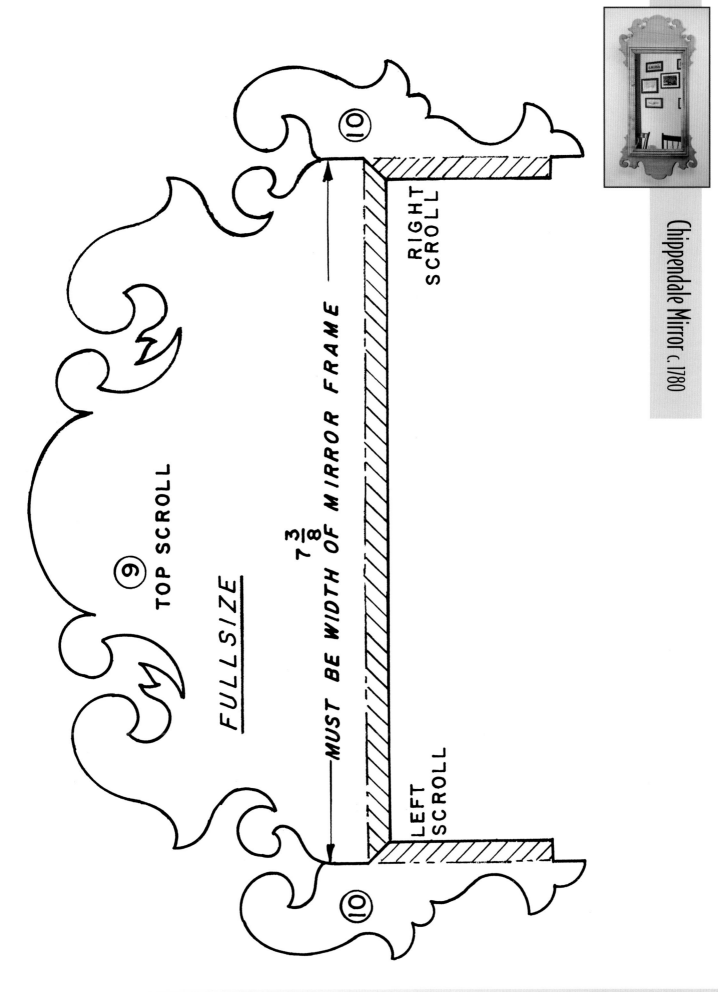

9 TOP SCROLL

FULLSIZE

10

10

RIGHT SCROLL

LEFT SCROLL

$7\frac{3}{8}$

MUST BE WIDTH OF MIRROR FRAME

Chippendale Mirror c. 1780

Chippendale Mirror
c. 1790

A dark stain makes this dramatic mirror cut from maple come to life. Note the flame scrolls on the upper left and right sides of this Chippendale-style mirror.

Materials List: Chippendale Mirror – c. 1790

No.	Name	Size	Pieces
1	Frame, Side	3/4" x 11/16" – 12 1/2"	2
2	Frame, Top/Bottom	3/4" x 11/16" – 8 3/4"	2
3	Spline	1/8" x 1 1/2" – 3"	4
4	Mirror	7 1/2" x 11 3/8"	1
5	Backing	1/4" x 7 1/2" – 11 3/8	1
6	Brace, Large	1/4" x 1/2" – 2 1/2"	4
7	Brace, Small	not required	
8	Nail, Square Cut	3/4" long	8
9	Top Scroll	1/4" x 5 1/2" – 9"	1
10	Side Scroll	1/4" x 1 1/4" – 4 1/4"	2
11	Bottom Scroll	1/4" x 3 1/4" – 9"	1
12	Side Scroll	1/4" x 1 1/2" – 4"	2

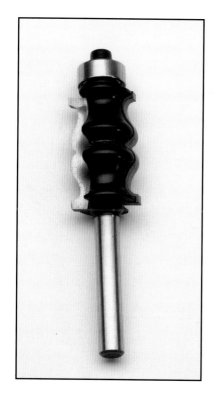

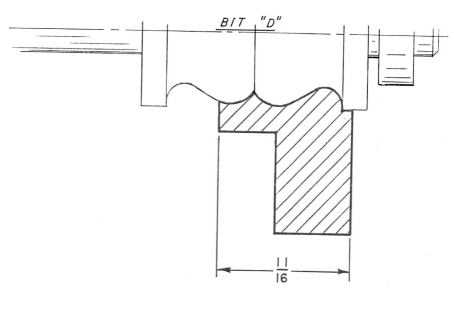

BIT "D"

11/16

Red line = Wood
Black line = Bit

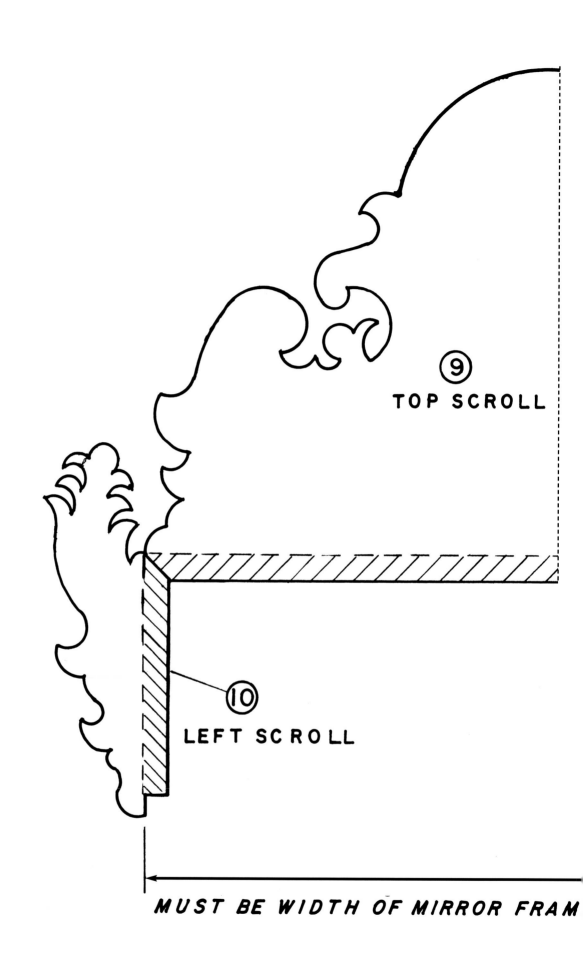

⑨
TOP SCROLL

⑩
LEFT SCROLL

MUST BE WIDTH OF MIRROR FRAM

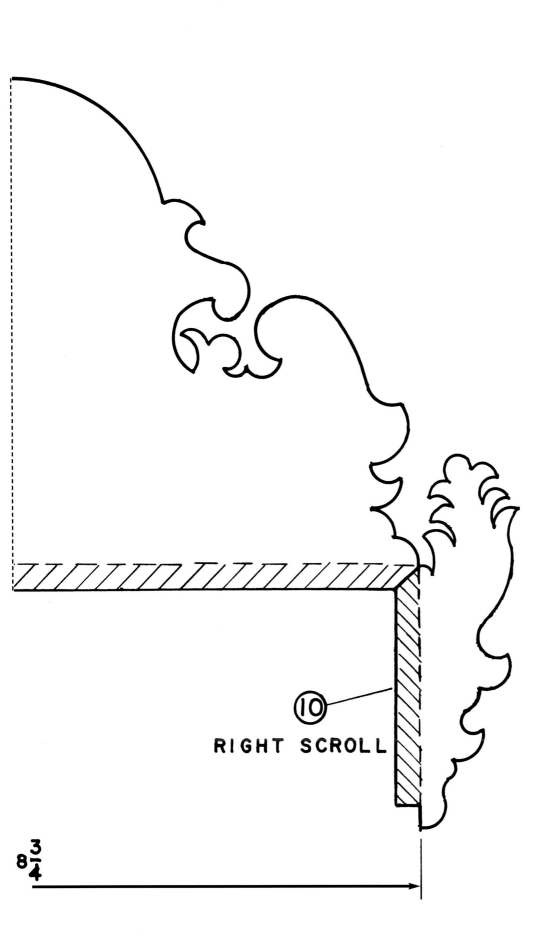

⑩

RIGHT SCROLL

$8\frac{3}{4}$

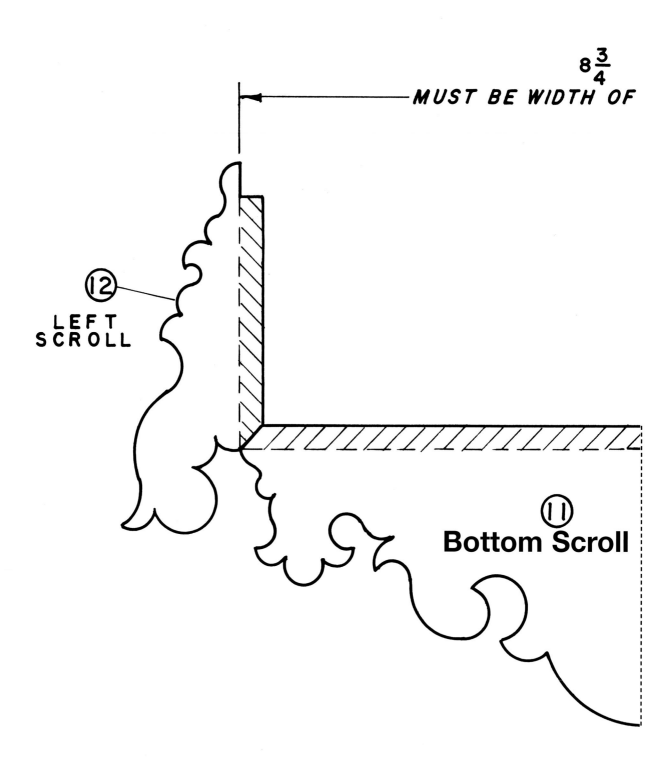

$8\frac{3}{4}$
MUST BE WIDTH OF

⑫
LEFT
SCROLL

⑪
Bottom Scroll

MIRROR FRAME

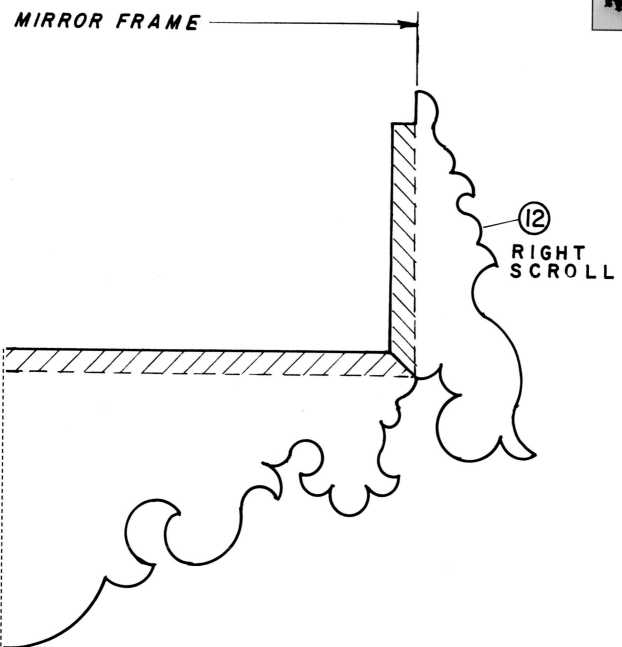

⑫
RIGHT
SCROLL

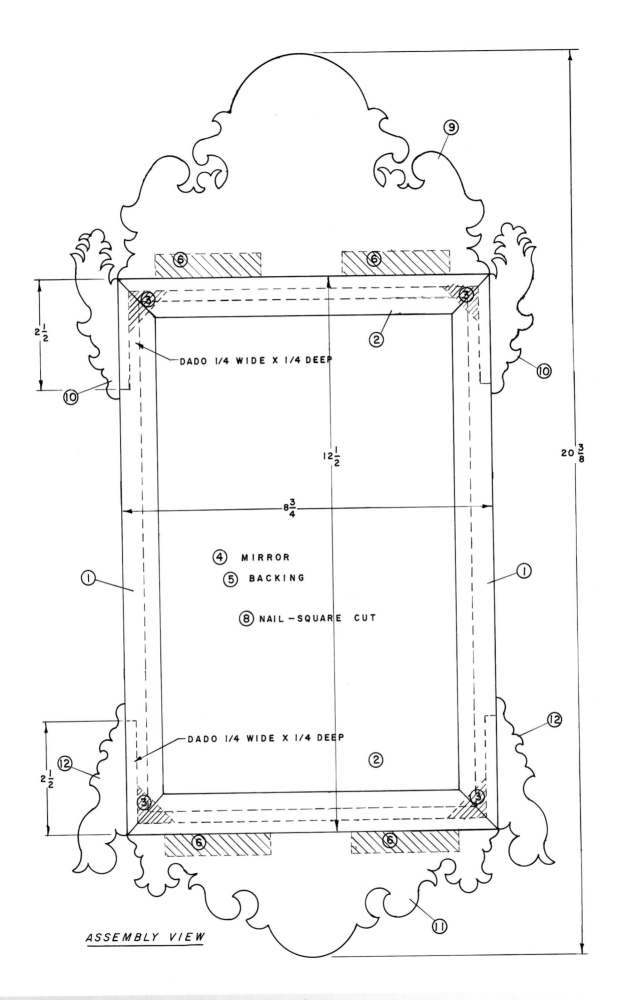

DADO 1/4 WIDE X 1/4 DEEP

$2\frac{1}{2}$

$12\frac{1}{2}$

$8\frac{3}{4}$

$20\frac{3}{8}$

④ MIRROR

⑤ BACKING

⑧ NAIL – SQUARE CUT

DADO 1/4 WIDE X 1/4 DEEP

$2\frac{1}{2}$

ASSEMBLY VIEW

Flaming Wall Mirror
c. 1780

Flames on the left and right sides enhance the look of this maple mirror. Created in the Chippendale style, this mirror is a circa 1780 reproduction.

Materials List: Flaming Wall Mirror – c. 1780

No.	Name	Size	Pieces
1	Frame, Side	$3/4"$ x $^{15}/_{16}"$ – $14"$	2
2	Frame, Top/Bottom	$3/4"$ x $^{15}/_{16}"$ – $9^3/_8"$	2
3	Spline	$1/8"$ x $1^1/_2"$ – $3"$	4
4	Mirror	$8^7/_8"$ x $12^5/_8"$	1
5	Backing	$1/4"$ x $8^7/_8"$ – $12^5/_8"$	1
6	Brace, Large	$1/4"$ x $1/2"$ – $2^1/_2"$	4
7	Brace, Small	not required	
8	Nail, Square Cut	$3/4"$ long	8
9	Top Scroll	$1/4"$ x $5^1/_4"$ – $9^1/_2"$	1
10	Side Scroll	$1/4"$ x $1^1/_2"$ – $4"$	2
11	Bottom Scroll	$1/4"$ x $3^3/_4"$ – $9^1/_2"$	1
12	Side Scroll	$1/4"$ x $1^1/_4"$ – $3^1/_2"$	2

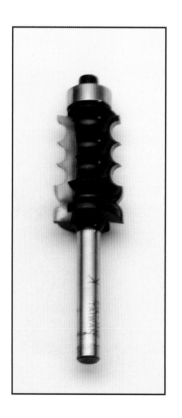

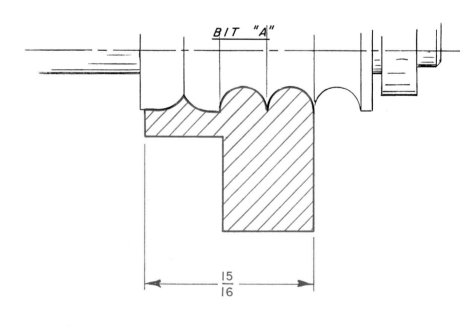

BIT "A"

$\frac{15}{16}$

Red line = Wood
Black line = Bit

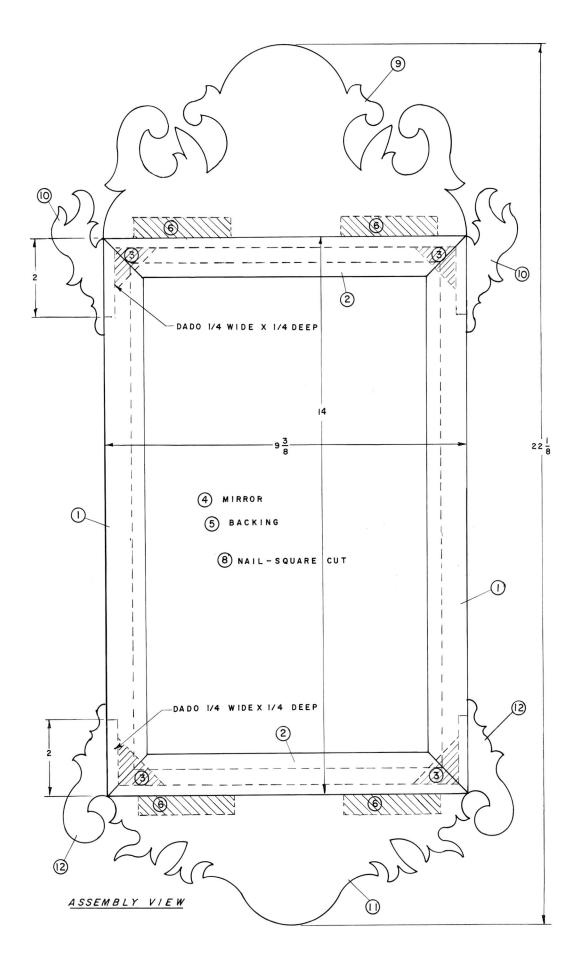

DADO 1/4 WIDE X 1/4 DEEP

2

14

9 3/8

22 1/8

④ MIRROR

⑤ BACKING

⑧ NAIL—SQUARE CUT

DADO 1/4 WIDE X 1/4 DEEP

2

ASSEMBLY VIEW

Flaming Wall Mirror c. 1780

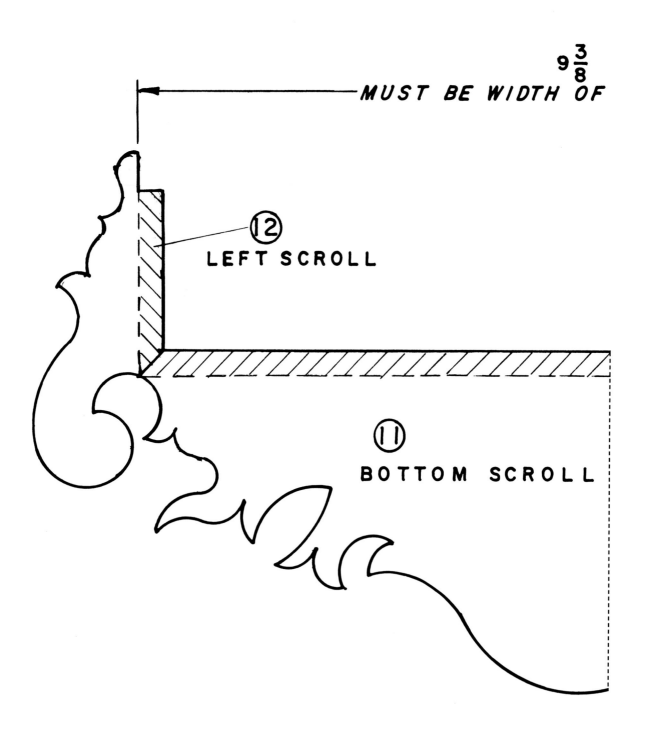

$9\frac{3}{8}$

MUST BE WIDTH OF

⑫ LEFT SCROLL

⑪

BOTTOM SCROLL

MIRROR FRAME

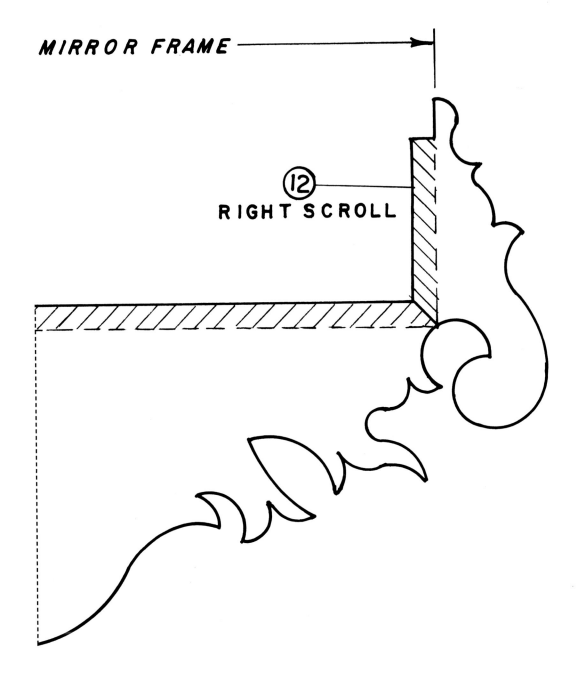

⑫
RIGHT SCROLL

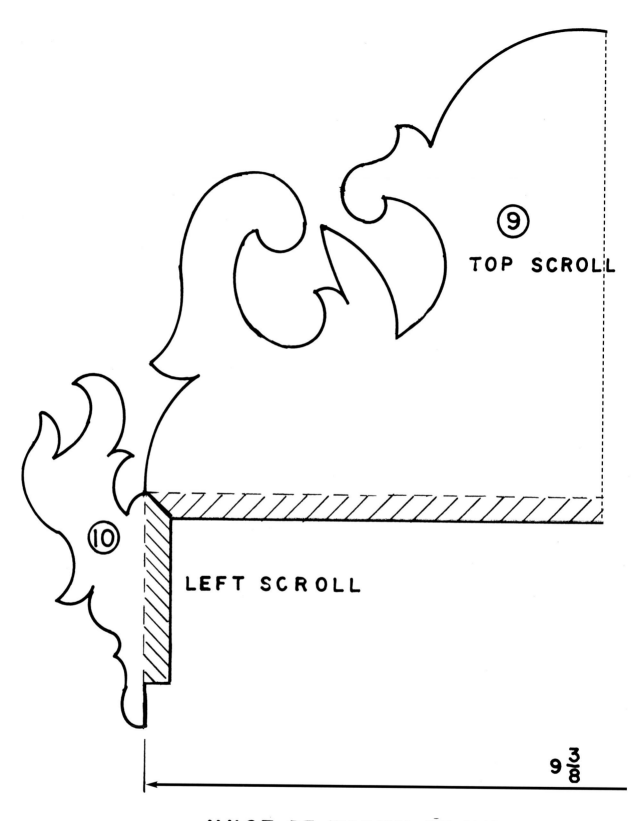

⑨
TOP SCROLL

⑩

LEFT SCROLL

$9\frac{3}{8}$

MUST BE WIDTH OF MIRROR FRAME

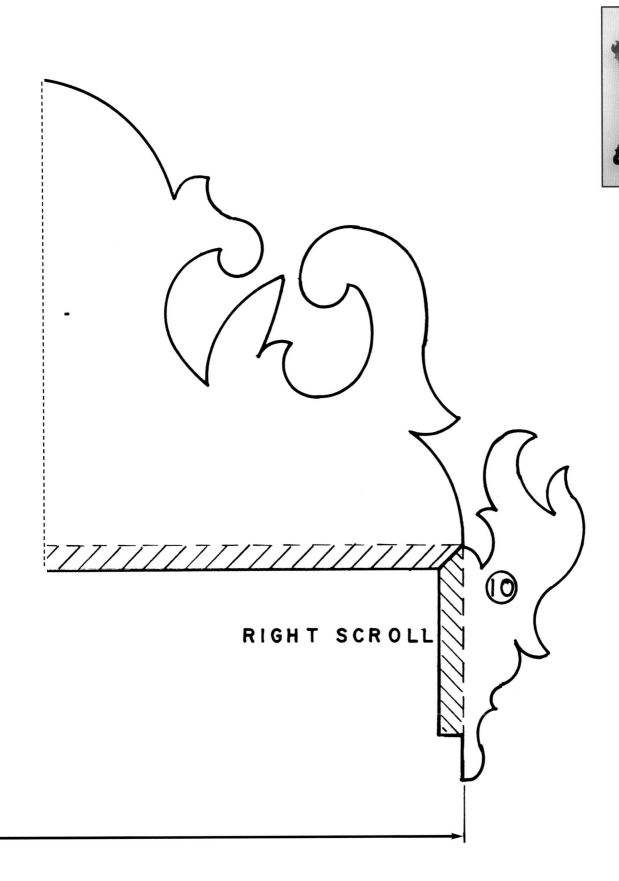

RIGHT SCROLL

Chippendale Wall Mirror
c. 1875

A later-style Chippendale mirror features mitered corners. This mirror is cut from tiger maple.

Materials List: Chippendale Wall Mirror – c. 1875

No.	Name	Size	Pieces
1	Frame, Side	3/4" x $^{15}/_{16}$" – 15"	2
2	Frame, Top/Bottom	3/4" x $^{15}/_{16}$" – 11$^{3}/_{8}$"	2
3	Spline	1/8" x 1$^{1}/_{2}$" – 3"	4
4	Mirror	9$^{7}/_{8}$" x 11$^{3}/_{8}$"	1
5	Backing	1/4" x 9$^{7}/_{8}$" – 11$^{3}/_{8}$"	1
6	Brace, Large	1/4" x 1/2" – 2$^{1}/_{2}$"	4
7	Brace, Small	1/4" x 1/2" – 1$^{1}/_{4}$"	4
8	Nail, Square Cut	3/4" long	8
9	Top Scroll	1/4" x 5$^{3}/_{8}$" – 13"	1
10	Side Scroll	1/4" x 1$^{5}/_{8}$" – 4$^{1}/_{4}$"	2
11	Bottom Scroll	1/4" x 3" – 13"	1
12	Side Scroll	1/4" x 2$^{1}/_{4}$" – 6$^{1}/_{2}$"	2

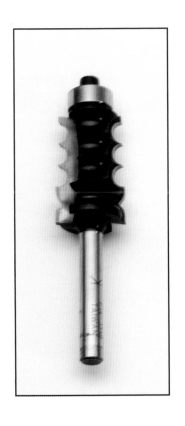

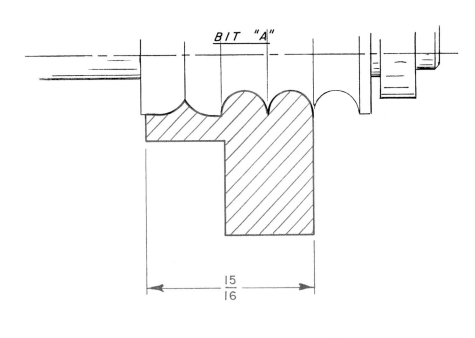

BIT "A"

$\frac{15}{16}$

Red line = Wood
Black line = Bit

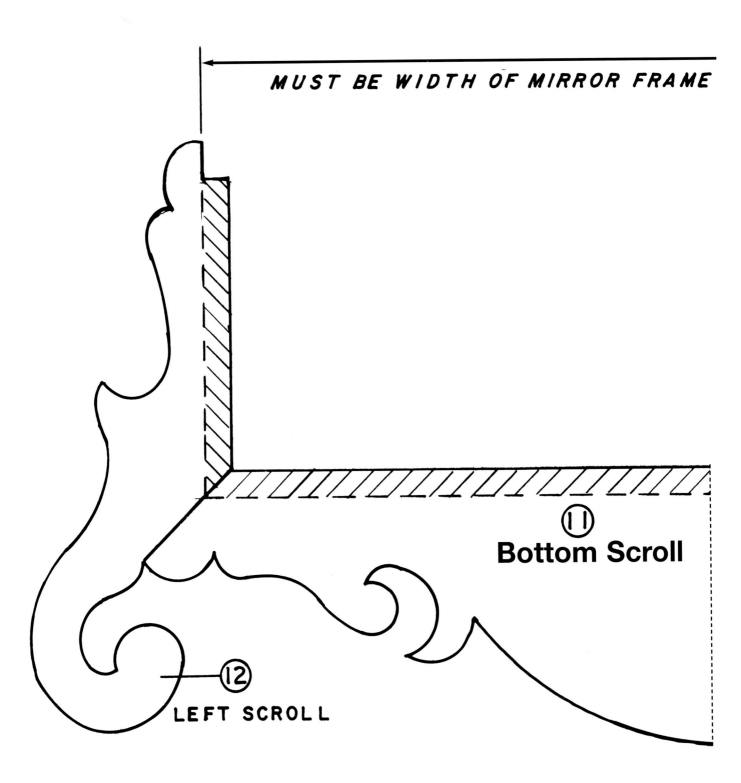

MUST BE WIDTH OF MIRROR FRAME

⑪
Bottom Scroll

⑫

LEFT SCROLL

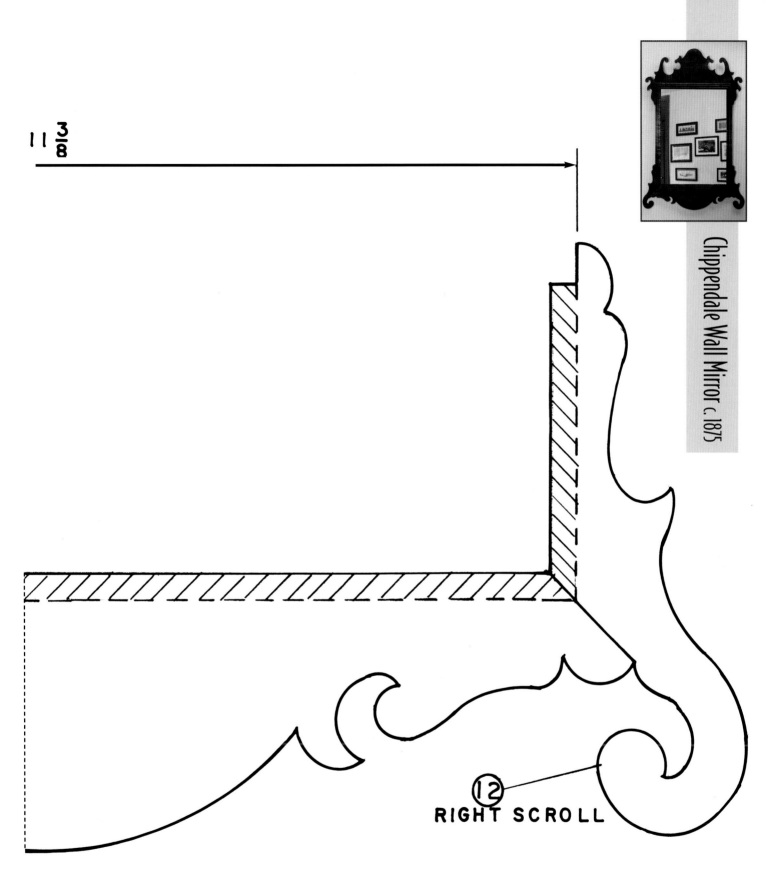

11 $\frac{3}{8}$

Chippendale Wall Mirror c. 1875

⑫
RIGHT SCROLL

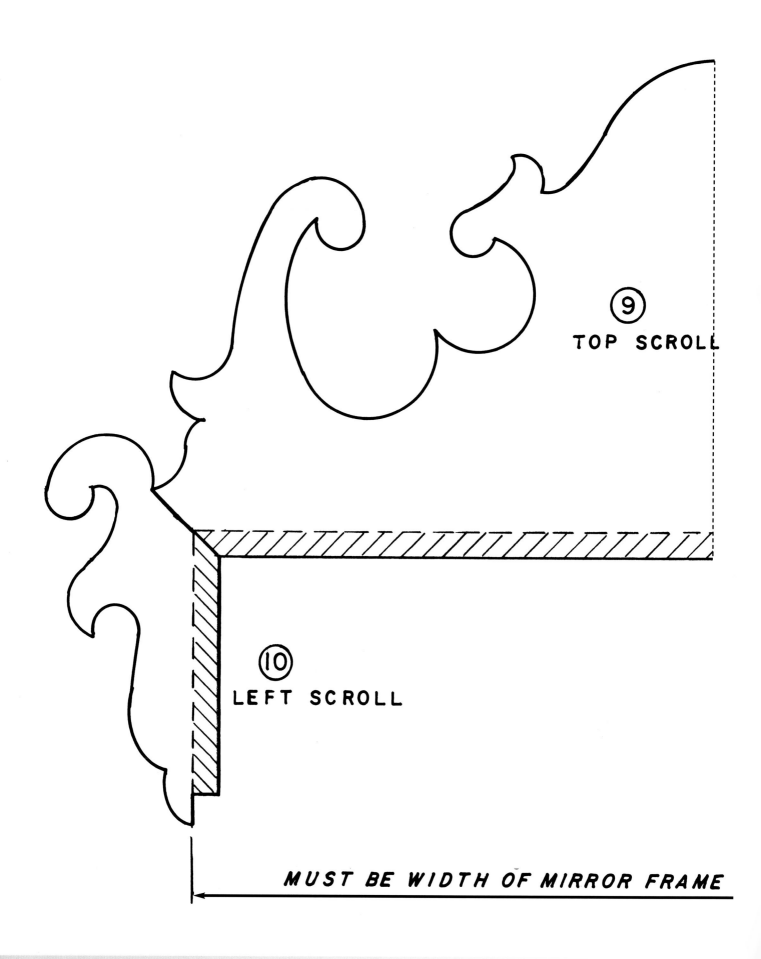

⑨ TOP SCROLL

⑩ LEFT SCROLL

MUST BE WIDTH OF MIRROR FRAME

⑩
RIGHT SCROLL

$11\frac{3}{8}$

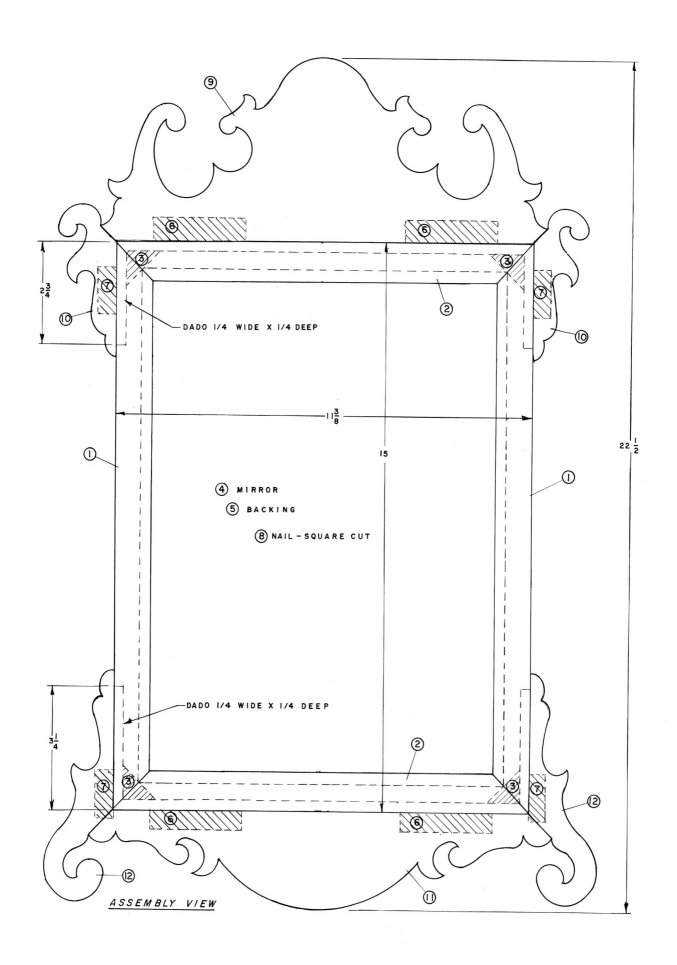

DADO 1/4 WIDE X 1/4 DEEP

2 3/4

11 3/8

15

22 1/2

④ MIRROR

⑤ BACKING

⑧ NAIL – SQUARE CUT

DADO 1/4 WIDE X 1/4 DEEP

3 1/4

ASSEMBLY VIEW

Early American Mirror with Inlay
c. 1800

Inlay can be used to add interest to any mirror. Here inlay decorates the top scroll of an Early American-style tiger maple mirror.

Materials List: Early American Mirror with Inlay – c. 1800

No.	Name	Size	Pieces
1	Frame, Side	$3/4"$ x $1^1/8"$ – $16"$	2
2	Frame, Top/Bottom	$3/4"$ x $1^1/8"$ – $11^1/2"$	2
3	Spline	$1/8"$ x $1^1/2"$ – $3"$	4
4	Mirror	$10^7/16"$ x $14^3/4"$	1
5	Backing	$1/4"$ x $10^7/16"$ – $14^3/4"$	1
6	Brace, Large	$1/4"$ x $1/2"$ – $2^1/2"$	4
7	Brace, Small	$1/4"$ x $1/2"$ – $1^1/4"$	4
8	Nail, Square Cut	$3/4"$ long	8
9	Top Scroll	$1/4"$ x $11^1/2"$ – $5^3/4"$	1
10	Side Scroll	$1/4"$ x $1^3/4"$ – $5^1/2"$	2
11	Bottom Scroll	$1/4"$ x $11^5/8"$ – $4^1/2"$	1
12	Side Scroll	$1/4"$ x $2"$ – $5^1/4"$	2

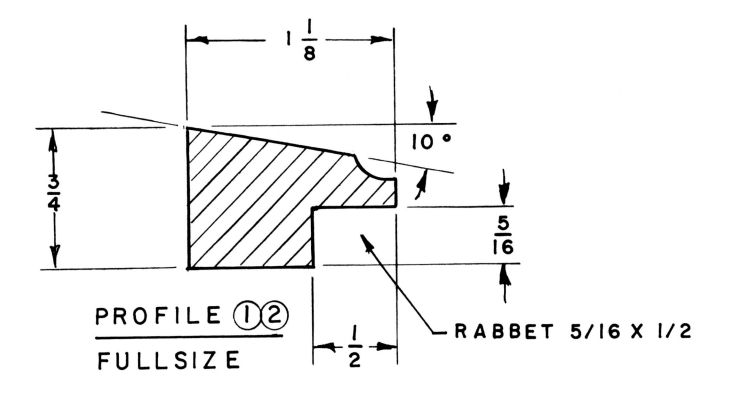

PROFILE ①②

FULLSIZE

RABBET 5/16 X 1/2

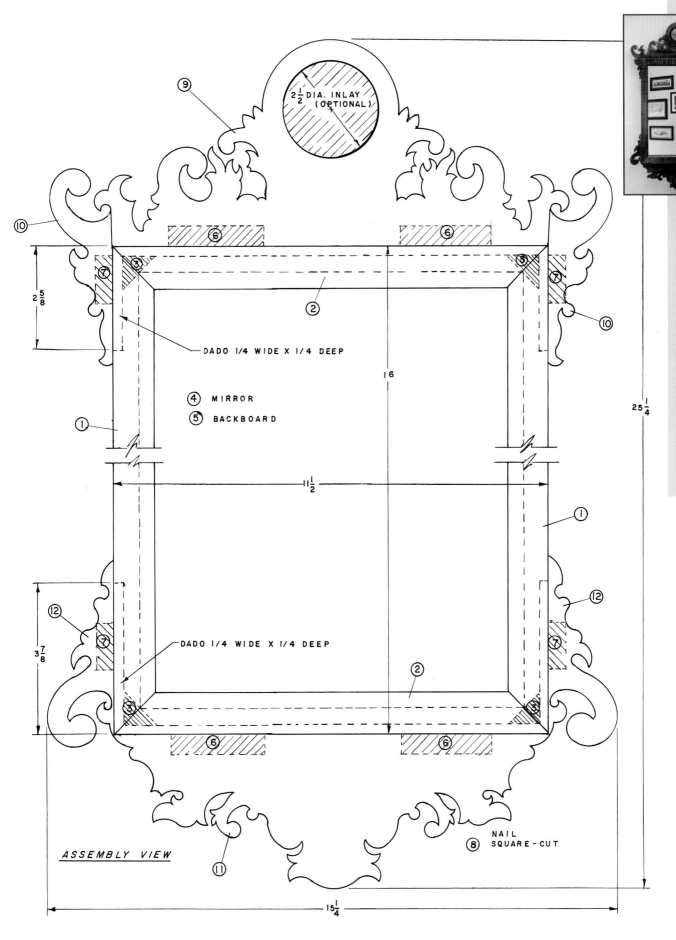

2½ DIA. INLAY
(OPTIONAL)

⑨

⑩

2⅝

DADO 1/4 WIDE X 1/4 DEEP

⑥   ⑥

⑦ ③   ③ ⑦

②

⑩

16

④ MIRROR

⑤ BACKBOARD

①

11½

⑫   ①

⑫

3⅞

⑦ DADO 1/4 WIDE X 1/4 DEEP   ⑦

②

③   ③

⑥   ⑥

NAIL
⑧ SQUARE-CUT

ASSEMBLY VIEW

⑪

15¼

25¼

$2\frac{1}{2}$

1/16 DEEP

DIA. INLAY

(Optional)

⑨

TOP SCROLL

$11\frac{1}{2}$

⑩

MUST BE WIDTH OF MIRROR FRAME

LEFT SCROLL

⑩

RIGHT
SCROLL

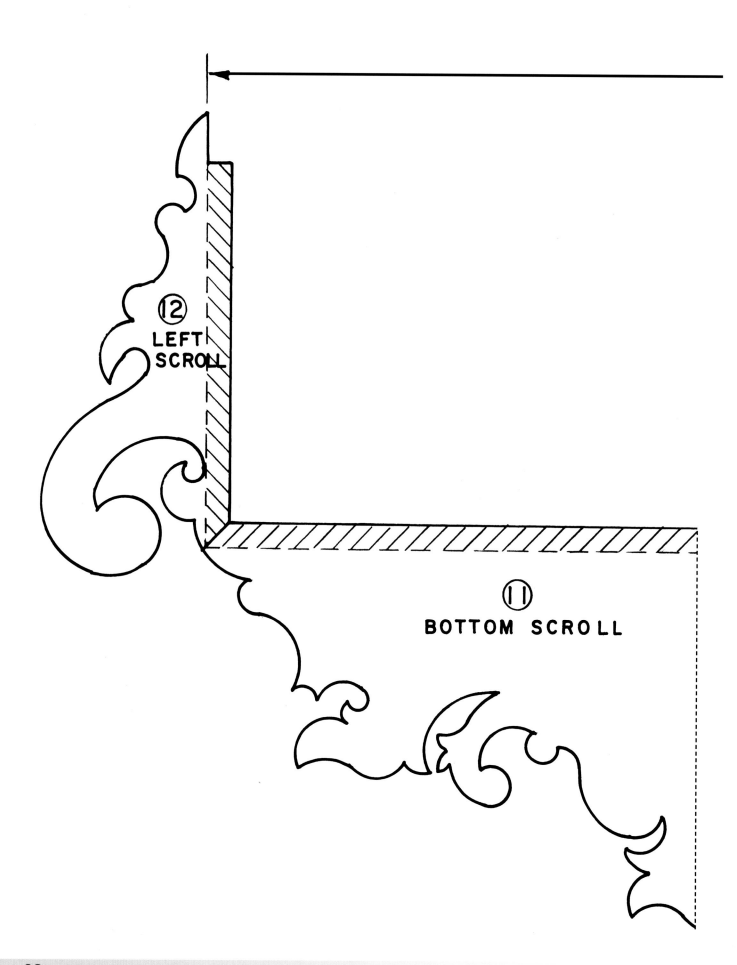

⑫
LEFT
SCROLL

⑪
BOTTOM SCROLL

$1\frac{1}{2}$ MUST BE WIDTH OF MIRROR FRAME

⑫ RIGHT SCROLL

Chippendale Wall Mirror
c. 1820

Large top and bottom scrolls plus side frames decorate this circa 1820 Chippendale-style mirror. The scrolls and the frame were cut from bird's eye maple.

Materials List: Chippendale Wall Mirror– c. 1820

No.	Name	Size	Pieces
1	Frame, Side	$\frac{3}{4}$" x $\frac{15}{16}$" – $12\frac{1}{4}$"	2
2	Frame, Top/Bottom	$\frac{3}{4}$" x $\frac{15}{16}$" – $10\frac{1}{8}$"	2
3	Spline	$\frac{1}{8}$" x $1\frac{1}{2}$" – 3"	4
4	Mirror	8 $\frac{3}{4}$" x 11"	1
5	Backing	$\frac{1}{4}$" x $8\frac{3}{4}$" – 11"	1
6	Brace, Large	$\frac{1}{4}$" x $\frac{1}{2}$" – $2\frac{1}{2}$"	4
7	Brace, Small	$\frac{1}{4}$" x $\frac{1}{2}$" – $1\frac{1}{4}$"	4
8	Nail, Square Cut	$\frac{3}{4}$" long	8
9	Top Scroll	$\frac{1}{4}$" x $5\frac{1}{2}$" – $10\frac{1}{2}$"	1
10	Side Scroll	$\frac{1}{4}$" x 2" – 5"	2
11	Bottom Scroll	$\frac{1}{4}$" x $3\frac{1}{2}$" – $10\frac{1}{2}$"	1
12	Side Scroll	$\frac{1}{4}$" x $1\frac{1}{2}$" – $4\frac{1}{2}$"	2

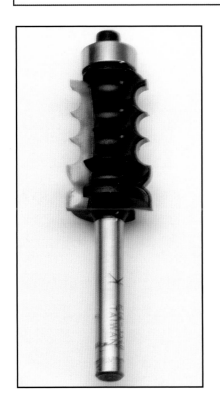

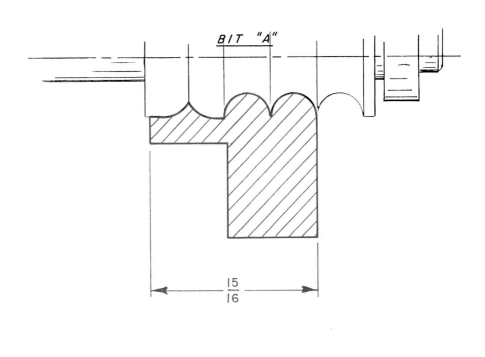

Red line = Wood
Black line = Bit

$10\frac{1}{8}$

MUST BE WIDTH OF MIRROR FRAME

⑫ LEFT SCROLL

⑪ TOP SCROLL

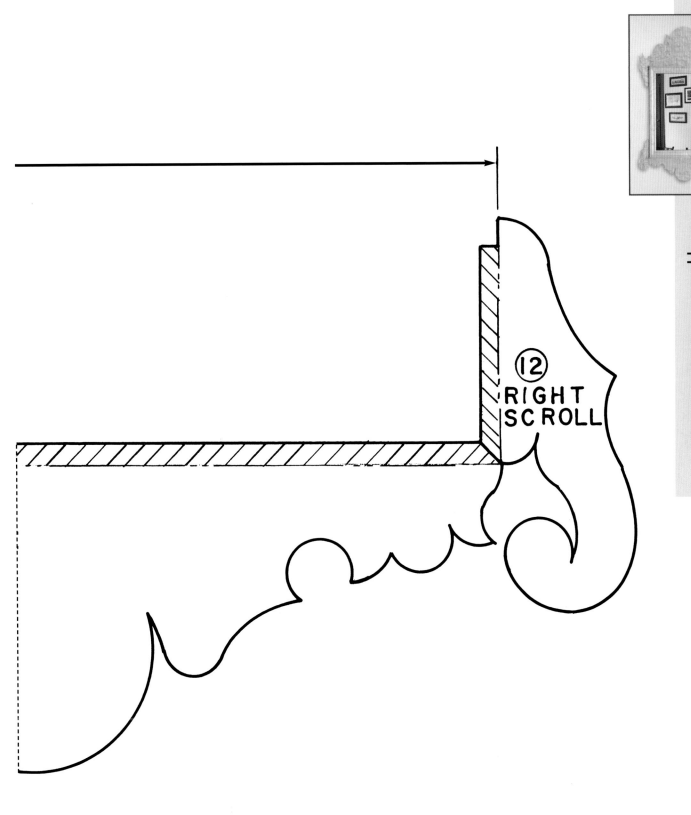

⑫
RIGHT
SCROLL

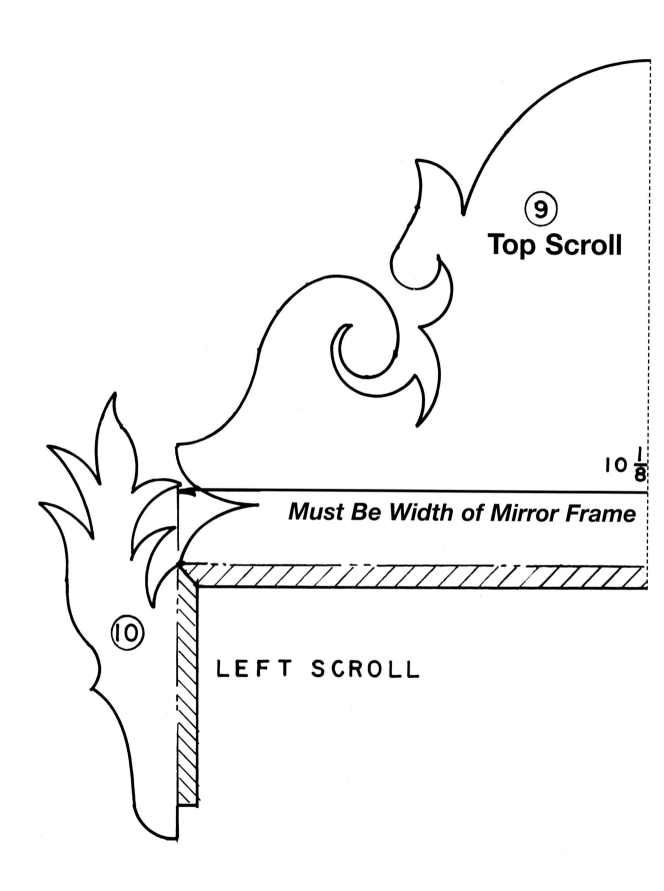

⑨
Top Scroll

$10\frac{1}{8}$

Must Be Width of Mirror Frame

⑩

LEFT SCROLL

⑩

RIGHT
SCROLL

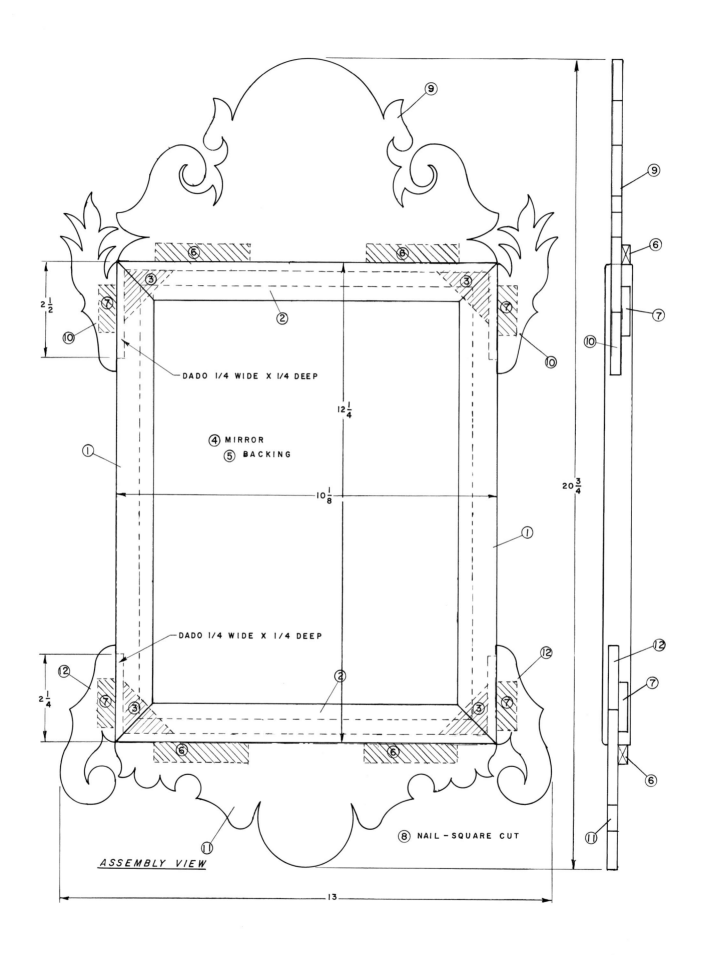

DADO 1/4 WIDE X 1/4 DEEP

② ④ MIRROR ⑤ BACKING

$12\frac{1}{4}$

$10\frac{1}{8}$

DADO 1/4 WIDE X 1/4 DEEP

$2\frac{1}{2}$

$2\frac{1}{4}$

$20\frac{3}{4}$

⑧ NAIL — SQUARE CUT

ASSEMBLY VIEW

13